The Day the Rabbi Disappeared

Jewish Holiday Tales of Magic

retold by Howard Schwartz
illustrated by Monique Passicot

VIKING

ALSO BY HOWARD SCHWARTZ

Next Year in Jerusalem: 3000 Years of Jewish Stories
Ask the Bones: Scary Stories from Around the World

For Shira
Nathan and Miriam

and for Tsila
with thanks
—H. S.

For Miau Miau
—M. P.

ACKNOWLEDGMENTS

Some of these stories have previously appeared in *Cricket,* the *Learn Torah With* series, *Judaism, Spider,* and *Tikkun.*

Special thanks to my editor, Deborah Brodie, who guided this book from its inception.

Thanks, too, to Arielle North Olson, Marc Bregman, and Vered Hankin for assistance in the editing of these stories.

Thanks also to Yocheved Herschlag Muffs, Judaica consultant, and to Janet B. Pascal, copy editor.

"Drawing the Wind" was written in collaboration with Arielle North Olson.

A recording of some of the stories in this book by storyteller Vered Hankin is available. For more information, please contact veredstory@hotmail.com.

VIKING
Published by the Penguin Group
Penguin Putnam Books for Young Readers, 345 Hudson Street, New York, New York 10014, U.S.A.
Penguin Books Ltd, 27 Wrights Lane, London W8 5TZ, England
Penguin Books Australia Ltd, Ringwood, Victoria, Australia
Penguin Books Canada Ltd, 10 Alcorn Avenue, Toronto, Ontario, Canada M4V 3B2
Penguin Books (N.Z.) Ltd, 182-190 Wairau Road, Auckland 10, New Zealand

Penguin Books Ltd, Registered Offices: Harmondsworth, Middlesex, England

First published in 2000 by Viking, a division of Penguin Putnam Books for Young Readers.

3 5 7 9 10 8 6 4 2

Text copyright © Howard Schwartz, 2000
Illustrations copyright © Monique Passicot, 2000
All rights reserved

LIBRARY OF CONGRESS CATALOGING-IN-PUBLICATION DATA
Schwartz, Howard, date
The day the Rabbi disappeared: Jewish holiday tales of magic / retold by Howard Schwartz ; illustrated by Monique Passicot.
p. cm.
Summary : Retellings of twelve traditional tales from Jewish folklore featuring elements of magic and relating to holidays, including Rosh Hodesh, Sukkot, Tu bi-Shevat, and Shabbat.
ISBN 0-670-88733-1
[1. Fasts and feasts—Judaism—Folklore. 2. Jews—Folklore. 3. Folklore.] I. Passicot, Monique, ill. II. Title.
PZ8.1.S4 Dat 2000
398.2'089'924—dc21   99-042061

Printed in U.S.A.
Set in Centaur MT

CONTENTS

INTRODUCTION

The story is told of a king who was about to sign an evil decree against the Jews. The people were terrified, but Rabbi Elimelech insisted they go ahead and celebrate the Sabbath as always. He said the Sabbath blessings. Then, before anyone began the meal, Rabbi Elimelech swept his arm across the table and knocked over a bowl of soup.

Later it was learned that at that very moment, just as the king was going to sign the decree, he accidentally knocked over the inkwell, spilling ink all over the parchment. The king took it as an omen. He tore up that evil decree and ordered that none like it should ever be drawn up again.

This tale recounts how a wise rabbi was able to save the Jewish community through magic. From a historical point of view, the story may well be a legend. But in the nineteenth century, people regarded it as a true account of a great sage who was famous for his magical powers.

The kind of magic Rabbi Elimelech uses in this story is known as sympathetic magic. Using it, a person can directly affect something that happens elsewhere, even at a great distance. This is only one of many kinds of magic found in this collection of tales.

Note that in the story, Rabbi Elimelech proceeds with the ritual of the Sabbath despite the danger. The Jewish people believe they are closest to God during the holy days—including the Sabbath—and it is essential, from the Jewish point of view, to maintain this close contact with the Divine. Indeed, during the most important of these holidays, Rosh Hashanah and Yom Kippur, a person's life is said to hang in the balance, as the decision is made in Heaven whether the person's name will be inscribed and sealed in the Book of Life.

Sometimes these tales of magic are linked with specific Jewish holidays. In this collection, one tale has been included for each of ten important holidays, as well as for Rosh Hodesh and the Sabbath. The first story is linked to Rosh Hodesh, the first day of the month, and the last story is linked to the Sabbath, the last day of the week. Readers wanting to know more about these holidays will find information following the stories.

Holidays serve an important role in these stories. Every holiday is a time of heightened awareness and closeness to God, but as these stories attest, they could be times of great danger as well. Then rabbis take on the role of sorcerers and come to the rescue, as did Rabbi Elimelech in the tale of the bowl of soup.

Indeed, Rabbi Elimelech, who came from the city of Lizensk in Poland, was one of a long line of Jewish sorcerers going all the way back to Moses. When Moses held his staff over the Red Sea (also known as the Sea of Reeds), the waters of the sea parted (Exodus 14:21). So, too, when Moses struck a rock with his staff, water came forth (Numbers 20:11). It is not hard for us to look at that staff as a kind of magic wand, and the parting of the sea as a kind of magic. But in this case, of course, the source of the magic is God.

Perhaps the greatest Jewish sorcerer of all was King Solomon, who knew the languages of the birds and even of the winds. He had a magic ring with God's name on it, which gave him unlimited powers, and a magic carpet that took him wherever he wanted to go.

King Solomon served as the model for all Jewish sorcerers who came after him. Among them were Rabbi Adam, who once moved a palace hundreds of miles in the blink of an eye, and Rabbi Judah Loew, who created the Golem, the man made of clay, which he brought to life by pronouncing God's secret name.

Jewish tradition holds that there is a secret pronunciation of God's four-letter name, YHVH. It is said that there is only one great sage in every generation who knows how to truly pronounce this name, and whoever knows this secret has unlimited powers at their command. Indeed, Jews do not pronounce God's name when it appears in prayers, out of concern that someone might accidentally pronounce God's name in the right way, and who knows what would happen then? Instead, they say *Adonai* (God) or *Ha-Shem* (the Name).

But God is not the only name with magic powers. There also are secret names of angels that, when pronounced, are the keys to magical feats. Indeed, angels are often found in these magical stories. Four angels give Rabbi Hanina ben Dosa a ride to Jerusalem, along with a beautiful stone he brings as a gift to the Temple. And Rabbi Hayim Pinto calls upon Rahab, the Angel of the Sea, to recover a treasure lost in a shipwreck.

So, too, are there remarkable tales about heavenly journeys, where rabbis ascend on high to study the secrets of Jewish mysticism. And there are mysterious figures who appear and serve as guides in times of great danger, such as the old man in "The Cottage of Candles" who watches over everyone's soul candle until it goes out and the soul takes leave of this world.

Another mysterious figure appears in "The Enchanted Menorah." Here the Baal Shem Tov dreams about Mattathias, the father of the Maccabees, who lived two thousand years ago, only to awake and find Mattathias waiting to guide him home in a blizzard. Dreams, in fact, are among the primary ways that God communicates with people in these stories. In "The Angel of Dreams," Rabbi Or Shraga asks a dream question before he goes to sleep. When the Angel of Dreams can't reach the rabbi, his wife receives the dream instead.

Still another kind of magic is used by Rabbi Nachman of Bratslav in "The Souls of Trees." After waking from a nightmare, he uses the mystical technique of opening a holy book at random and pointing to a passage, which serves not only to interpret his dream, but also to explain why the innkeeper and his wife have remained barren.

Yet even though these rabbis function as sorcerers, they know well that the complete source of their power comes from God, and from their unshakable faith in God. And even though they have great powers, their aim is not to accomplish supernatural effects for their own benefit, but only to promote the well-being of the Jewish people. Indeed, from this perspective, what occurs in these stories is not so much magic as miracles of God. This is the essence of Jewish magic, for ultimately the Jewish people depend on God and not on magic to guard and protect them.

A FLOCK OF ANGELS
A Rosh Hodesh Tale

Long ago, in the Kurdish town of Mosul, there lived a young woman named Asenath who was known for performing wonders. Her blessings were often sought by women who wished to have babies, or by sick people who wished to be cured. Her touch had healing powers, especially for children.

Asenath had learned everything from her father, Rabbi Samuel Barzani, who was well acquainted with the secrets of Heaven. He had taught these secrets to her until her wisdom and powers were as great as his own. It was whispered among the people that the spirit of her father rested upon her, and for this reason she was known as Rabbi Asenath.

After Rabbi Samuel died, he often came to his daughter in dreams. He would reveal dangers to her and tell her how to ward them off, saving many lives. One night Asenath dreamed that Rabbi Samuel told her to go to the Kurdish town of Amadiyah for Rosh Hodesh, the celebration of the new moon. He told her that the Jews of Amadiyah needed her protection.

When it became known that Rabbi Asenath was planning to travel to Amadiyah, the people of her town pleaded with her not to go, for things had become dangerous for the Jews living there. "All Jews have been warned to stay away from Amadiyah," they warned her. "If you go, you will surely be risking your life!" But Asenath had made up her mind. She bid farewell to the people of her town and began her journey.

When Rabbi Asenath reached the town that she had visited so often, she was given great respect as a holy woman. But the people were upset when she told them that they should celebrate Rosh Hodesh outdoors, so they could see the crescent of the new moon, as was their custom. They wanted to stay in the safety of the synagogue, for they knew they were surrounded by enemies and that their very lives were in danger. "Don't be afraid," she told them. And their faith in God and their trust in her were so great that they agreed to proceed as in the past, despite the danger.

So on the night of Rosh Hodesh, all the people came out to celebrate the new moon and the new month. At first they were cautious, yet soon they were singing and dancing in the town square with abandon. But suddenly there were shouts and they saw flames shoot up into the sky. The synagogue had been set on fire! Thank God, no one had been inside it. Yet they could not bear to see their synagogue consumed in flames. Many men had to be held back so they wouldn't run inside and be burned to death while trying to save the Torah scrolls. Everywhere people wept, falling to their knees, for they knew the flames were fast approaching the Ark where the Torahs were kept.

At that very moment, Rabbi Asenath whispered a secret name, one that she had learned from her father. All at once the people heard a loud flapping and a great wind swirled around them, and they thought that a flock of birds must be overhead. But when they looked up, they saw a flock of angels descending to the roof of the synagogue. The angels beat the flames with their wings, until every last spark had been put out. Then they rose up into the heavens like a flock of white doves and were gone.

The people were awestruck. They cried out, "Angels! Angels!" And when the smoke cleared, they saw that another miracle had taken place: the synagogue had not burned. Nor was a single letter of any of the Torahs touched by the flames.

When the enemies of the Jews learned of the miracle of the angels and saw how the synagogue had been saved from the fire, they were so fearful that they dared not harm the hair of even a single Jew.

As for the Jews of that town, they wept and prayed and thanked God for saving them and their beloved synagogue. And they were so grateful to Rabbi Asenath that they renamed the synagogue after her, and it is still standing to this day.

And all this came to pass because of Rabbi Asenath's courage and loyalty in honoring her father's wish, conveyed in a dream, that she go to that town for the celebration of the new moon.

Kurdistan, seventeenth century

ABOUT

"A FLOCK OF ANGELS"

Rosh Hodesh

Rosh Hodesh marks the beginning of a new Jewish month. The new month begins when the new moon appears. In Biblical times, months were calculated by the moon, and Rosh Hodesh was a minor festival. Special offerings were made, and the shofar, the ram's horn, was sounded, as written in Psalms 81:4: *Sound the shofar on the new moon . . . for the festive day.* In talmudic times, the beginning of a new month was declared when two witnesses saw the crescent of a new moon and reported it to the Sanhedrin, the high court. They relayed this information by lighting signal fires on hilltops.

Jewish legend records that God made Rosh Hodesh a special day for women, to reward them for refusing to help their husbands build the golden calf at Mount Sinai. It was traditional for women not to work on this day. In recent years, Jewish women have rediscovered Rosh Hodesh as a time to celebrate the rebirth and renewal of women and the moon. They also choose Rosh Hodesh for a naming ceremony for baby daughters or as a time to meet for religious and educational purposes.

Rabbi Asenath Barzani

Until the modern era, very few women were given the title of "Rabbi." But sometimes a woman's wisdom and learning were so exceptional that this title was given to her. Such is the case with Rabbi Asenath Barzani, who lived in Mosul, Kurdistan, from 1590 to 1670. Another instance was Hannah Rochel Werbermacher, known as the Maid of Ludomir, who lived in Eastern Europe in the nineteenth century and was also recognized as a rabbi. Rabbi Asenath was the daughter of Rabbi Samuel Barzani, who headed many yeshivas (schools for Jewish students) during his lifetime, and whose authority in Kurdistan was absolute. He was a master of Kabbalah, the Jewish mystical tradition, and he was said to have taught many of its secrets to his daughter.

After Rabbi Barzani died, many Jews made pilgrimages to his grave in Amadiyah. His daughter adored her father, whom she regarded as a king of Israel. He was her primary teacher, and after his death she took over many of his duties. Not only did Asenath serve as a rabbi, but she became the head of the Yeshivah of Mosul, and eventually became known as the chief teacher of Torah in Kurdistan. In addition, she was a poet and an expert on Jewish literature, and there are many Kurdish legends about the miracles she performed, such as the one described in "A Flock of Angels."

DRAWING THE WIND
A Rosh Hashanah Tale

Long ago, on the Spanish island of Majorca, a young boy spent most of each day at the shore, sketching the ships that sailed into the harbor. Solomon was a wonderful artist, everyone agreed. His drawings seemed so real that people wondered if the waves in his pictures were as wet as they seemed—or the sun as hot.

His father was a great rabbi who really preferred Solomon to spend his time studying, but Solomon would always slip away to the shore.

A few days before Rosh Hashanah, the Jewish New Year, a ship arrived from the city of Barcelona. Solomon overheard one of the sailors talking to a local merchant.

"There's news from Spain that will make every Jew on this island tremble."

"What is it?" asked the merchant.

"The king and queen have decreed that all the Jews in the land must give up their religion and become Christian."

"And if they refuse?"

"Then they must leave at once," said the sailor.

"But what if they want to stay?"

"Then they lose their lives."

Solomon was frightened. He didn't want to leave his beautiful island. He ran home to tell the news to his father, Rabbi Simeon ben Tsemah Duran.

"Must we leave, Father?" asked Solomon.

"I cannot leave, my son," said his father. "The other Jews look to me for guidance. I must stay until they all escape. But you should go, and I will join you later in Algiers."

"I won't leave you," said Solomon. "You are all I have since Mother died. Surely God will protect us."

Rabbi Simeon hugged his brave son. "Then let us work together and spread the word that everyone must meet in the synagogue." They hurried through the village, knocking at the doors of every Jewish home and shop.

When everyone had gathered at the house of prayer, Rabbi Simeon told them about the terrible decree.

"Save us!" they cried out in fear.

They hoped their beloved rabbi would work a miracle. For they knew his prayers had once turned back a plague of locusts. Another time, when crops were withering in the fields, his prayers had brought rain.

"You have only three choices," Rabbi Simeon told the men. "You can escape by sailing to Algiers. You can stay and pretend to convert, but secretly remain a Jew. Or you can defy the king and queen. As for me, I would rather go to my grave than say that I am giving up my religion." Solomon realized how strong his father was and how Rabbi Simeon strengthened and comforted his people.

In the days that followed, most of the Jews crowded onto ships, carrying very little with them. They saw to it that the women and children took the first available ships. Some Jews stayed and pretended to convert, in order to save their lives. They were known as *Conversos*, but in secret they continued to follow their Jewish ways.

Only a handful of Jews openly refused to convert. Among them were Solomon's father and Solomon himself. They planned to leave together, once they were certain that all those who wished to escape had done so.

By then it was the start of Rosh Hashanah. Rabbi Simeon and Solomon and those few who dared to enter the synagogue prayed with great intensity that year, in hope that their names would be written in the Book of Life. For Rosh Hashanah is when that decision is said to be made. Surely God would hear their prayers and guard them.

All went well the first day, but on the second day of Rosh Hashanah, just after the sounding of the shofar, soldiers rushed into the synagogue and dragged them all away. They were cast into a prison cell, where Rabbi Simeon continued to lead the prayers for Rosh Hashanah by heart. Solomon would have been terrified if he hadn't seen how calm his father remained.

None of them slept that night. Even though Rosh Hashanah had ended, they stayed awake, praying. The cell was very dark, with only one high window. But at dawn it let a little sunlight in. When Rabbi Simeon saw it, he said, "Have faith, my brothers. For just as there is a bit of light, so there is hope, and I feel that God has heard our prayers and will protect us."

The guard overheard them and laughed. "You think you have hope? You have just three days to live. Then you die. Let's see what your God does for you then."

Rabbi Simeon saw how frightened they were. So he turned to Solomon and said, "Won't you help us pass the time? Why don't you draw one of those ships you do so well?"

Solomon couldn't believe his ears. His father was asking him to draw? Solomon felt in his pocket and pulled out his last piece of chalk. When he looked up, he thought he saw a hint of a smile on his father's face.

Solomon remembered all the ships he had watched from the shore, and he began to draw the one he thought was the most beautiful on the sunlit wall. He drew the wind that filled the great sails, and he added barrels of wine and bushels of wheat.

Solomon's father and the other men watched him draw until the sun set and the prison cell was enveloped in darkness. Then they began to pray to God to save them. Once again, they prayed all night long.

The next day, Solomon continued to work on his drawing. Little by little he finished every detail of the ship, and then he drew the sea around it. The waves looked as if they might spill right off the wall and splash onto the floor.

The picture seemed finished, but Solomon didn't want to stop. His father suggested that he draw the two of them, there on the deck. This Solomon did, and all the men marveled at the fine resemblances he drew. Then the second day in

prison ended, and again they prayed throughout the night.

When the sun rose on the third day, one of the men asked Solomon to draw him on the ship, too. "For I would like to be with you." And one by one, the others made the same request. But when darkness fell, Solomon had not finished drawing the last man.

That night they prayed to God with all their hearts, for they knew the execution was set for sunrise the next day. All of the men shook with fear, except for Rabbi Simeon. Solomon took strength from his father, and he, too, remained unafraid.

As soon as the first light of dawn came through the window, Solomon took out his chalk and quickly finished drawing the last man.

Just as he drew the final line, he heard keys jangling. The soldiers were coming to unlock the door to their cell. Then Solomon and all the men would be taken to the courtyard for their execution.

Solomon turned to his father and saw that he was deep in prayer. And, at that very moment, he heard his father pronounce God's secret name out loud.

Suddenly Solomon could not hear the guards in the hallway, and when he looked down, he saw that he was standing on the deck of the beautiful ship he had drawn on the prison wall.

His father and all the other men in the picture were with him, safely aboard a real ship floating on a real sea. The sails strained against the wind, just as they had in Solomon's drawing, and the ship sped away from danger.

All the Jews from the prison cell rejoiced with Solomon and his father—for they knew they were aboard a ship of miracles, on their way to freedom. They would never forget that Rosh Hashanah, the Day of Judgment, when God had seen fit to save them.

The Balkans, oral tradition

ABOUT
"DRAWING THE WIND"

Rosh Hashanah

Rosh Hashanah, the Jewish New Year, takes place on the first day of the Hebrew month of Tishre (in September or October). Traditionally, it represents the birthday of the world. It starts a ten-day period known as the Days of Awe, which concludes on Yom Kippur, the Day of Atonement. Starting on Rosh Hashanah, Jews examine their lives, to see if they are living up to their own ideals and those of their religion. It is also a time for making amends to those who have not been treated fairly, so that the new year can be started with a clean slate.

It is believed that on Rosh Hashanah a decision is made in heaven whether or not a person will live another year. That is why it is known as the Day of Judgment. Although this decision is made on Rosh Hashanah, it is not sealed until Yom Kippur, ten days later. It is possible, during this period, to reverse the decree by repentance, prayer, and acts of charity. That is why it is said that "the gates of repentance are always open" (Deuteronomy Rabah 2:12 and Lamentations Rabah 3:15). On Rosh Hashanah the shofar is sounded in the synagogue, and it is considered an obligation for all Jews to be present to hear it.

The Expulsion

In 1492, King Ferdinand and Queen Isabella signed a decree expelling all Jews from Spain. Jews who did not convert to Christianity or leave were sentenced to death. This decree included people living on the Spanish island of Majorca. Hundreds of thousands of Jews were expelled from

Spain and went into exile in many countries, especially in the lands of the Middle East. Of those Jews who remained, many pretended to convert, but secretly carried out Jewish rituals. These people are known as *Conversos* or *Marranos.* If they were caught in the broad net of the Spanish Inquisition, they were tortured and executed. Thousands of Jews lost their lives. Even so, many persisted in remaining secret Jews. To this day there are Catholic Spaniards who practice certain Jewish rituals, such as the Sabbath blessing over bread and wine, although they no longer remember why. They are descended from those *Conversos.*

Rabbi Shimon ben Tsemah Duran

Rabbi Simeon (Shimon) ben Tsemah Duran, the leader of the Jewish community of Majorca in the fourteenth and fifteenth centuries, was highly respected as a rabbinic scholar. He also was a physician and surgeon with a vast knowledge of mathematics, astronomy, and science.

Although Rabbi Simeon was born in 1361 and died in 1444, before the Expulsion took place in 1492, he was such a towering presence that legend has placed him in Majorca during the Inquisition that followed, as in this tale. In reality, Rabbi Simeon and his family left Majorca for Algiers after a massacre that took place in 1391. There, Rabbi Simeon continued to be recognized as one of the great leaders of his time.

The Tetragrammaton

The secret name of God that Rabbi Simeon pronounces in this story is known as the Tetragrammaton. It was believed that whoever knew how to pronounce this name had great powers. King Solomon is said to have used the power of the Name to capture Ashmodai, the king of demons. And Rabbi Judah Loew of Prague is said to have used it to bring to life the Golem, a man made of clay. According to Jewish tradition, only one great sage in each generation knows the secret pronunciation.

THE COTTAGE OF CANDLES
A Yom Kippur Tale

There once was a Jew who went out into the world to seek justice. He saw how people mistreated each other, and how hard they were on the animals. Surely, he thought, the world was not that harsh everywhere. Somewhere, he was certain, true justice must exist, but he had never found it. So he set out on a quest that consumed most of his years. He went from town to town and village to village searching for justice. But never did he find it.

In this way many years passed, until the man had explored all of the known world except for one last, great forest. He entered that dark forest without hesitation, for by now he was fearless. He went into the caves of thieves, but they mocked him and said, "Do you expect to find justice here?" And he went into the huts of witches, but they laughed and said, "Do you expect to find justice here?"

Now, it happened that the man lost track of time in his wanderings. At sunset on the eve of Yom Kippur, the Day of Atonement, he arrived at a little clay hut that looked like it was about to collapse. Through the window he could see many flickering flames, and he wondered why they were burning. He knocked on the door, but there was no answer. As he waited, he noticed that the whole forest had grown silent. Not a single bird sang. He knocked again. Nothing. At last he pushed the door open and stepped inside.

As soon as he entered that cottage, the man realized that it was much larger on the inside than it had seemed to be from the outside. He saw that it was filled with hundreds of shelves, and on every shelf there were dozens of oil candles. Some of those candles were in precious holders of gold or silver or marble, and some were in cheap holders of clay or tin. Some of the holders were filled with oil and the flames burned brightly. But others had very little oil left, and it seemed that they were about to sputter out.

All at once an old man stood before him. He had a long, white beard and was wearing a white robe. "*Shalom aleichem*, peace be with you, my son," the old man said. "How can I help you?" The man who sought justice replied, "*Aleichem shalom*, with you be peace. I have gone everywhere searching for justice, but never have I seen anything like this. Tell me, what are all these candles?"

"Each of these candles is the candle of a person's soul," said the old man. "As long as that person remains alive, the candle continues to burn. But when that person's soul takes leave of this world, the candle burns out."

"Can you show me the candle of my soul?" asked the man who sought justice. "Follow me," the old man said, and he led the way through that labyrinth of a cottage, which appeared to be endless. At last they reached a low shelf, and there the old man pointed to a candle in a holder of clay. The wick of that candle was very short, and there was very little oil left. The old man said, "That is the candle of your soul."

Now, the man took one look at that flickering candle, and a great fear fell upon him. Was it possible for the end to be so near without his knowing it? Then he happened to notice the candleholder next to his own. It was full of oil, and its wick was long and straight and its flame burned brightly. "And whose candle is that?" the man asked.

"I can only reveal each man's candle to himself alone," the old man said, and he turned and left.

The man stood there, staring at his candle, which looked as if it was about to burn out. All at once he heard a sputtering sound, and when he looked up, he saw a wisp of smoke rising from another shelf, and he knew that somewhere, someone was no longer among the living. He looked back at his own candle and saw that there were only a few drops of oil left. Then he turned to the candleholder next to his own, so full of oil, and a terrible thought entered his mind.

He stepped back and searched for the old man, but he didn't see him anywhere. So he lifted that oil candle, ready to pour it into his own. But all at once the old man appeared out of nowhere and gripped his arm with a grip like iron. And the old man said: "Is this the kind of justice you are seeking?"

The man closed his eyes. And when he opened his eyes, he saw that the old man was gone, and the cottage and all the candles had disappeared. He found himself standing alone in the forest and heard the trees whispering his fate. He wondered, had his candle burned out? Was he, too, no longer among the living?

Afghanistan, oral tradition

ABOUT
"THE COTTAGE OF CANDLES"

Yom Kippur

Yom Kippur, which takes place on the tenth of the Hebrew month of Tishre (in September or October), is the Day of Atonement, the holiest day of the Jewish year. Jews the world over mark it by praying and fasting, soul-searching and repenting, seeking God's forgiveness. For twenty-five hours all Jews, except for those who are too young or too ill, take no food or water. On Yom Kippur, a person's life is said to hang in the balance: will his or her name be sealed in the Book of Life for the year to come? It is a day to reconcile with God and with anyone we may have wronged in the preceding year. Yom Kippur is sometimes called "the Sabbath of Sabbaths," because it is such a special day. Like the Sabbath and all other holy days, it begins at sunset the night before and ends the next evening, at sunset. The prayers and melodies of Yom Kippur are

especially beautiful and moving, and the whole service and experience of
Yom Kippur can be exceptionally profound. At the end of Yom Kippur
the shofar is sounded, and those who have spent the day in fasting and
prayer come away with the hope that their names are inscribed and sealed
in the Book of Life.

The Sources of This Story

"The Cottage of Candles" is a perfect example of a folktale based on
Biblical verses. Consider the following: *Justice, justice shalt thou pursue*
(Deuteronomy 16:20) and *The soul of man is the candle of God* (Proverbs
20:27). Note how the first verse sets in motion the quest that propels the
story, and how the second is the focus of the climactic episode about the
cottage of candles. This story was told in the harsh land of Afghanistan,
where justice is still hard to find. It is not difficult to imagine how the
Biblical verses that serve as the foundation of this tale inspired it, for
surely the longing for justice in a place like Afghanistan could easily lead
to such a tale.

Behind almost every Jewish tale, there is some Biblical concept or
episode or verse. For example, the next story, "Four Who Entered
Paradise," alludes to the journey of Elijah into Paradise in a fiery chariot at the end of his life (2 Kings 2:11), while the story told in the Bible
in the Book of Esther hangs over everything that happens in "The Angel
of Dreams."

The Keeper of the Soul Candles

The identity of the old man in this story remains a mystery. The Keeper
of the Soul Candles functions as an Elijah-like figure who is hidden in
the forest. Perhaps he is one of the *Lamed-Vav Tzaddikim*, the thirty-six hidden saints who are said to serve as the pillars of the world. God is said
to sustain the world because of their presence. Or he might be viewed as

the Angel of Death. Perhaps he is even God. The fact that the story takes place at Yom Kippur suggests that the old man might well be God, who judges the man who seeks justice on the Day of Judgment.

Divine Tests

Many of the most important stories in the Bible are divine tests, such as that of Adam and Eve and the forbidden fruit, or the binding of Isaac, or the suffering of Job. "The Cottage of Candles" is another example of such a divine test. The man seeking justice attempts to fulfill the Biblical injunction *Justice, justice shalt thou pursue* by setting out on a quest to find justice.

Such quests are quite common in Jewish tales and in general folklore, too, although they are rarely this abstract. Usually, they are a quest for something such as a golden bird, a lost princess, or the sword of Moses. Each quest tests the character of the individual involved. Instead of proving worthy, the man who seeks justice attempts to lengthen his life at the expense of someone else's, but he is caught and pays the price. In this sense he does find justice, for justice is exactly meted out.

The Jewish Idea of Justice

The concept of justice as found in the American Declaration of Independence is directly linked to the Jewish ideal, as stated in the verse *Justice, justice shalt thou pursue.* This pursuit of justice serves as the model not only for democratic nations, but for the peoples of nations living under dictatorships, who long for the day when they will find justice as well. In this context, "The Cottage of Candles" might be seen as a folk meditation on the idea of justice. The moral of the story is clear: Those who seek justice need to search for it not only out in the world but also inside themselves.

FOUR WHO ENTERED PARADISE
A Sukkot Tale

On the seventh and last night of Sukkot in the Moroccan town of Azmor, it was the custom to stay up until dawn, studying the mysteries of the Torah without interruption. It is said that the gates of heaven open for an instant during this night, and any wish made at this time will be fulfilled.

So it was that the leading sages of the city—Rabbi Shimon, Rabbi Reuven, and Rabbi Moshe—had gathered in Rabbi Yakov's sukkah, a booth covered with leaves, to study the very secrets of Jewish mysticism, known as Kabbalah.

Now, Rabbi Shimon had a daughter whose name was Yona, who accompanied her father to Rabbi Yakov's house. Yona was curious about what her father and the others were doing in the sukkah. So, late at night, when no one noticed, she left the house and peered inside. There she saw her father and the others deep in study. She watched them for a while and then returned to the house.

A little later Yona came back to the sukkah and looked inside again. This time the sukkah was empty. Yona could not understand where her father and the others had gone. Then she happened to glance at a silver plate hung in the sukkah, and in it she saw four pairs of eyes, which she recognized as those of her father and his friends!

Yona was terrified. How could they have disappeared? Where had they gone? And what was the meaning of the eyes she saw reflected in that silver plate? She could not stop trembling. She was about to run back into the house to tell the oth-

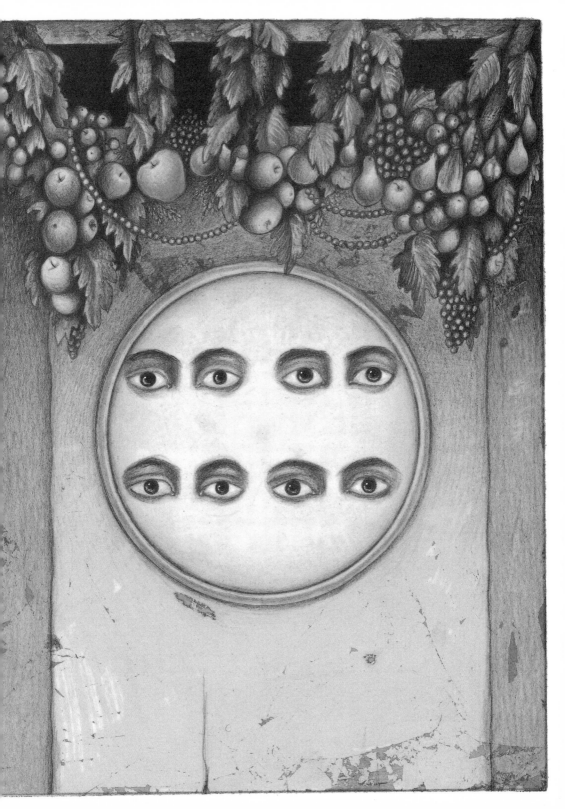

ers what had happened when suddenly the four rabbis appeared in the sukkah once more, and their eyes were no longer reflected in the plate.

Yona could not restrain herself and ran into the sukkah, crying. She embraced her father and clung tightly to him. Then she told him what she had seen and asked him what it meant. Rabbi Shimon replied: "Yona, I am very sorry you were so frightened. You see, we were studying the mysteries of Kabbalah when, all at once, the heavens parted, and an angel invited us to study Kabbalah in heaven. But because we are not allowed to look upon God, we left our eyes behind when we ascended on high. That is what you saw."

Morocco, oral tradition

ABOUT

"FOUR WHO ENTERED PARADISE"

Sukkot

Sukkot begins on the fifteenth of the Hebrew month of Tishre (in September or October) and ends seven days later. The seventh and final day of Sukkot, when this story takes place, is known as Hoshanah Rabbah. It is customary to stay up studying all night on Hoshanah Rabbah. In particular, the Zohar and other books of a mystical nature are read at that time, as happens in this story.

Sukkot is one of the three Jewish pilgrimage festivals, along with Passover and Shavuot. In ancient times, before the Temple in Jerusalem was destroyed, Jews in the land of Israel would try to make pilgrimages to Jerusalem on these days to bring harvest offerings to the Temple. Of these three festivals, Sukkot most retains the character of a harvest festival. The *lulav*, a palm branch, and the *etrog*, a citron fruit, are carried during Sukkot services. During the seven days of Sukkot, some Jews eat and sleep in booths known as *sukkot* that are erected beside their homes or synagogues, or on rooftops of apartment buildings, with only leafy boughs serving for the roof. This is to remind them of the wandering of the Israelites in the wilderness during the time of the Exodus, when the people had to live in temporary dwellings.

There is a kabbalistic tradition that the three Jewish patriarchs, Abraham, Isaac, and Jacob, together with Joseph, Moses, Aaron, and David, come to visit the sukkah on each night of the holiday. One of them is specifically welcomed on each of the seven nights. There is a new custom of also inviting the four matriarchs, Sarah, Rebekah, Rachel, and Leah, along with Miriam, Deborah, and Esther, or other female leaders, to visit in the sukkah.

The Four Who Entered Paradise

It is often possible to find the models for Jewish folk stories in earlier sources. Hasidic tales are often based on kabbalistic ones, and kabbalistic tales find their model in rabbinic tales, and at the bedrock of Jewish tradition is the Torah, from which almost all Jewish stories are ultimately drawn. The original heavenly journey was that of Elijah found in the Bible, where *a fiery chariot with fiery horses suddenly appeared . . . and Elijah went up to heaven in a whirlwind* (2 Kings 2:11).

This account was drawn upon by an ancient tale from the Talmud about four sages who entered Paradise. After they returned, Ben Zoma is said to have lost his mind, Elisha ben Abuyah to have lost his faith, and Ben Azzai to have lost his very life. Only Rabbi Akiba survived. This legend is a very mysterious one, and there are many opinions about what it means.

But it is clear that the story included here, "Four Who Entered

Paradise," which was collected in modern-day Israel, finds its source in the Talmudic model, although here all four rabbis ascend and descend in peace. The reason for their success may be that they learned from the errors of the ancient sages. In the Talmud it says that "Ben Azzai looked and died." Because it is forbidden to look directly at God, the four Moroccan rabbis avoided this danger by leaving their eyes behind; and in this way their lives were saved. Thus we see how a theme first found in the Bible is still being echoed in a tale collected orally in Israel during the last forty years.

Jewish Mysticism

Mystics long to have direct knowledge of God. Since Jews believe that God is in Heaven, they sought to find a way to travel to Heaven, so they could be closer to God. The four rabbis in this Moroccan story find the opportunity to go to Heaven on Sukkot, when the sky opens for an instant, and an angel invites them to study Kabbalah—Jewish mysticism—in Paradise. The fact that the four were invited to make this journey means their greatness had been recognized in Heaven, and that is why they were able to make such a blessed journey.

Rabbi Shimon Elkayam

Rabbi Shimon Elkayam, known as Rabbi Shimon the Hazan, since he was a cantor, served as a rabbi in the Moroccan town of Azmor from 1930 to 1949. As a child, he studied Torah in the city of Marrakesh. When he was twenty, he went back to Azmor and studied Torah with the rabbis of that city. Rabbi Shimon also studied Kabbalah and wrote twelve books, though none were published, and only one manuscript remains, in the hands of his son in Jerusalem. The other three sages who appear in the story are Rabbi Reuven Kohen, Rabbi Moshe Kohen, and Rabbi Yakov Rawami.

THE FLYING SHOE
A Simhat Torah Tale

Every year the followers of the Baal Shem Tov, known as Hasidim, celebrated Simhat Torah with wild dancing and singing. That is the joyous day when the reading of the Torah is begun anew, and Jews dance with the Torah in their arms.

Then one year his Hasidim noticed that the Baal Shem Tov did not join in the dancing, but stood off by himself. He seemed to be strangely somber on that joyful day. Suddenly a shoe flew off the foot of Rabbi Dov Baer as he whirled in the dance, and at that instant the Baal Shem Tov smiled.

A little later the Hasidim saw the Baal Shem Tov pull a handful of leaves out of his pocket, crush them, and scatter their powder in the air, filling the room with a wonderful scent, like that of Paradise. Then the Baal Shem Tov joined in the dancing with great abandon. The Hasidim had never seen him so happy, and they, too, felt possessed by a greater joy than ever before.

Afterward, when they had all caught their breath, one of the Hasidim asked the Baal Shem Tov what he had smiled about, after having been so solemn.

The Baal Shem Tov replied: "While you were dancing, I went into a trance, and my soul leaped from here into the Garden of Eden. I went there to bring back leaves from the Garden, so that I could scatter them among us, making this the happiest Simhat Torah of all time. I gathered fallen leaves with the greatest pleasure and put them in my pocket. As I did, I noticed that there were scattered fringes of prayer shawls in the Garden, as well as pieces of worn tefillin, from the straps Jews wrap

around their arm when they pray. Not only that, but I saw heels and soles and shoelaces, and sometimes even whole shoes. And all of these objects were glowing like so many sparks—even the shoes—for as soon as they entered the Garden of Eden, they began to glow.

"Now I was not surprised to see the fringes and straps, for they come from sacred objects, but I wondered what the shoes were doing there.

"Just then a shoe flew into the Garden of Eden, and I recognized it at once as that of Rabbi Dov Baer." The Baal Shem Tov turned to face him. "Dov, I realized that your love of God was so great that your shoe had flown all the way there. That is when I understood why there were shoes in the Garden of Eden. And that is why I smiled.

"I would have come back to join you at that very moment, but just then I saw two angels in the Garden. They had come to sweep and clean the Garden and to gather those precious, glowing objects.

"I asked the angels what they were going to do with the shoes, and one of them said: 'These shoes have flown here from the feet of Jews dancing with the Torah. They are very precious to God, and soon the angel Gabriel will make a crown out of them for God to wear on His Throne of Glory.'"

The Baal Shem Tov stopped speaking, and all who heard this story that day were filled with awe. Nor was Rabbi Dov Baer's shoe ever seen again, for it had truly flown to the Garden of Eden.

Eastern Europe, eighteenth century

ABOUT
"THE FLYING SHOE"

Simhat Torah

Simhat Torah follows the seventh day of Sukkot and is a day of rejoicing. On Simhat Torah, the year-long reading of the Torah comes to an end with the last few verses of the Book of Deuteronomy and starts again with the first verses of the Book of Genesis. The scrolls of the Torah are taken from the Ark and carried around the synagogue in a procession that makes seven circuits around the sanctuary. After each circuit, there is singing and dancing with the scrolls. It is a celebration of great joy for having lived to complete the reading of the Torah for another year. In some Hasidic circles, there is wild dancing, as in this tale.

The Baal Shem Tov

Rabbi Israel ben Eliezer, known as the Baal Shem Tov, "Master of the Good Name," was the founder of Hasidism. He was born in approximately 1700 and died in 1760. There are hundreds of miraculous legends about him, but very few facts about his life are known. He is said to have been an orphan who spent most of his time in the fields and forests and later served as a teacher's assistant. He studied Jewish texts on his own, but he kept his knowledge hidden until the age of thirty-six. Then he became known as a healer and *baal shem*, a miracle worker.

The Baal Shem Tov made his home in the Polish town of Medzhibozh, where he attracted many followers, known as Hasidim. This movement grew into a major spiritual revival in Judaism. The Baal Shem Tov emphasized the importance of *kavanah,* or intensity, in prayer, and dancing and singing as a way to come closer to God. His teachings also involved a revival of attention to Kabbalistic texts. His followers included Rabbi Dov Baer, who became his successor. The next story in this collection, "The Enchanted Menorah," is also about the Baal Shem Tov.

The Garden of Eden

The Garden of Eden *(Gan Eden)* represents Paradise on earth. It is first introduced in the book of Genesis, in the story of Adam and Eve. Adam and Eve were expelled from the Garden of Eden when they disobeyed God's command not to eat the fruit of the Tree of Knowledge. God then placed an angel with a flaming sword to guard the entrance of the Garden of Eden. Although the gates of the Garden were closed after this, there are quite a few visits to the Garden recounted in Jewish folklore, such as that of the Baal Shem Tov in this story. This shows how Jewish folktales draw on Biblical themes and retell them, perpetuating the influence of the Bible in Jewish tradition. Today the Garden of Eden symbolizes the idea of perfection, where there is harmony between nature and people.

THE ENCHANTED MENORAH
A Hanukkah Tale

A long time ago, before Rabbi Israel ben Eliezer became known as the Baal Shem Tov, he and his wife Hannah lived in the Carpathian Mountains. During the week, Rabbi Israel wandered by himself in the dense forests there. He loved nature and studied everything he saw, the deer and fawn, the birds and squirrels, and all the animals that were in the forest.

All week, during all kinds of weather, in summer or winter, he would walk alone and meditate among the trees. And on Friday, just before sundown, he would return home for the Sabbath.

During the week in which Hanukkah was to be celebrated, Rabbi Israel told his wife, "With God's help, I will return home on the eve of Hanukkah to light the first candle. But if I am late for some reason and haven't arrived before sundown, don't wait for me, but light the candle by yourself and put the Hanukkah menorah in the window."

On the afternoon of the eve of Hanukkah, just as Rabbi Israel was about to return home, it started to snow, and a strong wind arose. Soon a blizzard was raging. Rabbi Israel buttoned up his coat, leaned on his heavy staff, and tried to make his way through the storm. Darkness was falling, and for the first time in his life, Rabbi Israel was lost. He could not find the narrow path in the forest that led to his home.

He walked and walked but somehow always returned to the same place. Yet because of his trust in God, he did not lose faith. He was only upset that he would not be able to light the candles on the first night of Hanukkah.

Soon Rabbi Israel became exhausted. He sat down to rest on a large stone, and because he was so tired, he fell asleep. While he slept, an image appeared in his dream of a tall old man carrying a candle in his hand. "Who are you?" the sleeping rabbi asked. The old man replied, "I am Mattathias, the father of the Maccabees, and I have brought this candle for you." At that instant Rabbi Israel awoke, and he was able to make out the dim shape of a person walking before him through the swirling snow. That person held a menorah in his hand, with one candle burning, a menorah that looked very much like Rabbi Israel's own.

Rabbi Israel picked up his staff and started following the light of the flame. For what seemed hours, he never let it out of his sight. At last he saw that he was not far from the place where he walked on the Sabbath. As he came closer, he recognized the fields and trees and saw that he was approaching his own village. Then he saw his own house. And there was his Hanukkah menorah in the window, its first candle lit with a clear and bright flame.

Rabbi Israel's wife stood outside the house, wrapped in her heavy winter shawl, deeply worried about him. It was already past midnight, and she was afraid that something had happened to him in that terrible storm.

When Rabbi Israel appeared on the path, she ran to him and embraced him. "Thank God that you have come home alive!" she said. There were tears of happiness in her eyes. "When it was becoming dark," she said, "and you hadn't returned, I lit the first candle of Hanukkah by myself. But no sooner did I light it than the candle and menorah vanished from the window. I was terrified, for I was sure it must be a sign that you were in danger."

Then Rabbi Israel understood that Mattathias had taken the menorah from his window and used it to guide him back home. He told his wife about his dream, and about the silent figure who had guided him through the forest. Before they entered the house, he pointed to the window and she saw that the menorah had been restored to its place. The flame of the candle glowed brightly in the night.

Germany, oral tradition

ABOUT

"THE ENCHANTED MENORAH"

Hanukkah

Hanukkah, which begins on the twenty-fifth day of the Hebrew month of Kislev (in December), marks the victory of Judah Maccabee and his followers over the Syrian army in the second century B.C.E. The victory of the Maccabees preserved Judaism. Thus the story of Hanukkah is the struggle of the Jewish people to remain Jewish. After their victory, the Temple in Jerusalem, which the Syrians had defiled, was rededicated. A legend in the Talmud reports that a miracle took place. Although there was not enough oil to keep the Temple menorah lit for the eight days it would take to make new oil, nevertheless the oil lasted that long. For this reason, Hanukkah has become known as the "Festival of Lights."

To celebrate the victory, an eight-day festival was created. It is observed by lighting a candle on the first night of Hanukkah and adding an additional candle each night. These candles are held in a special Hanukkah menorah, called an *hanukkiyah*, the kind of menorah found in this story.

THE SOULS OF TREES
A Tu bi-Shevat Tale

One day Rabbi Nachman of Bratslav told his Hasidim to ask Lepke the coachman to prepare for a journey. When the Hasidim wondered where he was going, all Rabbi Nachman said was "We are needed somewhere."

Soon the coachman arrived, and Rabbi Nachman invited three of his Hasidim to join him. Then, just as they were about to depart, Lepke asked Rabbi Nachman where he wanted to go. Rabbi Nachman replied, "Hold the reins loosely, Reb Lepke, and let the horses go wherever they please." The coachman was surprised, but he did as the rabbi asked.

The Hasidim rode for many hours, while the horses took one road after another, proceeding as if they knew exactly where they were going. When the sun began to set, the Hasidim wondered where they would spend the night. At last one of them asked Rabbi Nachman, and all he replied was "God will provide."

Then, just as darkness was falling, the carriage reached an inn. Rabbi Nachman called out for the coachman to stop, and everyone got out.

The Hasidim had never been to this inn before, so they were delighted to find that it was run by a Jew and his wife. But before long they noticed that the innkeeper seemed to be very sad, though they dared not ask him what was wrong.

Now the innkeeper had heard of Rabbi Nachman and treated him with great respect and consideration. He and several other Jews who were staying at the inn joined Rabbi Nachman and the Hasidim for evening prayers. All together there were ten men, just enough to make a *minyan*. After the innkeeper's wife served a fine meal, the innkeeper showed the Hasidim to their rooms. But before he left Rabbi Nachman, he asked if he could discuss something with him in private.

"Surely," said Rabbi Nachman, and he offered the innkeeper a chair. When the man was seated, he told Rabbi Nachman his story: "My wife and I have been married for ten years, and we love each other deeply. But there is one sadness that fills our lives and overshadows everything else. For there is nothing in the world that we long for more than a child of our own. But so far God has not blessed us with a son or daughter. Rabbi, is there anything you can do to help us?"

Rabbi Nachman was silent for a long time. Then he said: "It is late and I am tired. Let me get a good night's sleep, and in the morning I will see if there is anything I can do for you." The innkeeper was pleased with this reply and took his leave of Rabbi Nachman.

Soon Rabbi Nachman and all the Hasidim were sound asleep. But in the middle of the night, Rabbi Nachman began to cry out loudly, waking up everyone in the inn. They came running to see what had happened.

When he awoke, Rabbi Nachman ignored all those who had gathered in his room wanting to know what was wrong. Instead, he picked up a book, closed his eyes, opened the book at random, and pointed to a passage. And there it was written, "Cutting down a tree before its time is like killing a soul."

Rabbi Nachman assured all those who had gathered there that he had recovered from his fright, and everyone could go back to sleep. "Let us rest," said Rabbi Nachman, "and in the morning we will speak." Everyone went back to sleep, except for the innkeeper and his wife, for they longed to know what the rabbi would tell them.

After morning prayers, Rabbi Nachman turned to the couple and asked them if the walls of that inn had been built out of saplings that were cut down before their time. The innkeeper and his wife looked at each other, and then back at Rabbi Nachman. "Yes," said the innkeeper, "it is true. But how did you know?"

Rabbi Nachman took a deep breath and replied: "All night I dreamed I was surrounded by the bodies of those who had been slain. I was very frightened. Now I

know that it was the souls of the trees that cried out to me. And now, too, I know why you have remained childless."

"Rabbi," sighed the innkeeper, "I do not understand. What do the saplings have to do with our not having children?"

"You see," said Rabbi Nachman, "there is an angel called Lailah, the angel of conception. She is the one who delivers the soul of the unborn child. But each time Lailah approaches your inn to bring you the blessing of a child, she is driven back by the cries of the souls of the trees that were cut down before their time."

"Oh, Rabbi, that is terrible," said the innkeeper. "Is there anything we can do?"

"Yes," said Rabbi Nachman. "You must plant trees all around this inn—twice as many trees as were cut down to build it. You must let them grow and take care that none of them are cut down. After three years, if the new trees have remained untouched, you will be blessed with a child."

The couple was overjoyed to hear this. That very day, even before Rabbi Nachman and his Hasidim took their leave, they began planting.

All the trees that the couple planted grew tall and strong. And after three years, Lailah returned to their home. The lullaby of the living trees quieted the cries of the trees that had been cut down, so that Lailah was able to reach the couple's house, tap on their window, and bless them with a child.

Lailah came back to the couple's home six more times. And every year that she did, the innkeeper's wife gave birth, until they were the parents of seven children, all of whom grew straight and tall as fine trees.

Eastern Europe, nineteenth century

ABOUT
"THE SOULS OF TREES"

Tu bi-Shevat

Tu bi-Shevat, which takes place on the fifteenth day of Shevat (in January or February), is the New Year for Trees. This holiday celebrates God and God's creations. On this day it is customary to eat foods from Israel that grow on trees, especially almonds and the fruit of carob trees. Some people celebrate by holding a Tu bi-Shevat Seder. This ritual was created in the sixteenth century by Kabbalists living in Safed in Israel.

In modern Israel, Tu bi-Shevat is a time for planting trees. Planting trees was considered so important by the rabbis that Rabbi Yohanan ben Zakkai taught, "If you are planting a tree and you see the Messiah coming . . . finish planting the tree and then go greet the Messiah." Folk tradition holds that, on Tu bi-Shevat, trees lean over and kiss each other. Almond trees, which are the first trees to blossom in Israel, are the ones most closely associated with Tu bi-shevat. Although this story, "The Souls of Trees," does not take place on Tu bi-shevat, it emphasizes both the sacred quality of trees as living beings and the importance of planting them.

The Sacredness of Trees

This story suggests that trees, like human beings, have souls, and therefore they must be treated with care and consideration. It is interesting to note that the Bible also compares people to trees, as in the passage *For*

Man is the tree of the field (Deuteronomy 20:19). In the Psalms, a person's life is again directly compared to that of a tree: *And he shall be like a tree planted by the rivers of water, that brings forth fruit in its season* (Psalms 1:3). In fact, there is such great respect for trees that the Torah itself is compared to a tree: *It is a tree of life to those who cling to it* (Proverbs 3:18). According to Jewish law, newly planted trees and any fruits they produce are to be left alone for three years, until it is clear that the tree is strong enough to survive.

Rabbi Nachman of Bratslav

Rabbi Nachman of Bratslav was one of the most important Hasidic rabbis. He was the great-grandson of the Baal Shem Tov, the founder of Hasidism, and is widely considered to be the greatest Jewish storyteller of all time. During his lifetime in the late eighteenth century, he had a small but devoted circle of followers, known as the Bratslav Hasidim, who believed that he had great wisdom and trusted him entirely to guide their lives. Rabbi Nachman used many methods to teach his Hasidim, including the telling of stories. He was not only sensitive to humans but also to the presence of spirits and, as we see in this story, even to the souls of trees.

Before his death, Rabbi Nachman told his followers that they would not need to appoint a new rabbi after he died, for he would always be their rabbi. They followed his instructions, although it was a Hasidic custom to appoint a new rabbi when the old one died. Even to this day, the Bratslav Hasidim are thriving in Israel and the United States, and they still follow the teachings of Rabbi Nachman.

Jewish Divination

Divination seeks to look into the future in order to decide a matter of importance. The Bible clearly states that any kind of divination is forbidden: *There shall not be found among you any one who makes his son or daughter to pass through the fire, one who uses divination, a soothsayer, or an enchanter, or a sorcerer, or a charmer, or one who consults a ghost or familiar spirit, or a necromancer. For whosoever does these things is an abomination unto the Lord* (Deuteronomy 18:10–12).

Nevertheless, various methods of divination were practiced by the Jewish people. Even in the Bible, King Saul goes to the Witch of Endor and has her call up the ghost of the prophet Samuel, so that Saul might ask him a question (I Samuel 28). It is also believed that the High Priest in the Temple in Jerusalem used the precious gems on his breastplate to perform divination.

In this story, Rabbi Nachman seeks the meaning of his dream by opening a book at random and pointing to a passage. This is a method of Jewish divination known as *she'elat sefer*. The book most commonly used for this kind of divination is the Bible, but the book that Rabbi Nachman consults refers to a passage from the Talmud: *Cutting down a tree before its time is like killing a soul.* This gives him the essential clue to link his nightmare with the suffering of trees.

Although various kinds of oracles were popular in the past, modern Jews rarely use any kind of divination.

THE ANGEL OF DREAMS
A Purim Tale

For two years, the city of Yezd in the land of Persia was besieged by rebels opposed to the Shah. Everyone in the city was in danger. Just before the holiday of Purim, the rebels gained the upper hand, and it looked as if the city were about to fall. In desperation, the Shah called upon Rabbi Or Shraga and implored him to pray for the city. The Shah had always been good to the Jews, and Rabbi Shraga promised to do so.

That night Rabbi Or Shraga asked a dream question, hoping that heaven would reveal how he could protect the city from falling into the hands of the enemy. The rabbi slept deeply that night, but when he awoke in the morning, he could not remember a single dream. He was terribly disappointed. He had been certain that Heaven would send him a dream in reply to his question.

He was about to go to the house of study when his wife said to him, "You know, I had a strange dream last night."

"What!" exclaimed the rabbi. "What did you dream?"

"I dreamed that an angel came and knocked on the window above your bed," she replied, "but you were sound asleep, and the angel could not wake you. Then the angel came and knocked at my window, and I opened it and let the angel in. The angel told me that it was the Angel of Dreams, and that it had been sent by Heaven to deliver a message to you, but since it could not wake you, the angel delivered it to me instead."

"What did the angel say?" asked the amazed rabbi.

"It said I could only whisper the message to you." Then she whispered into his ear everything that the angel had revealed.

The next day, the day before Purim, Rabbi Or Shraga summoned all the elders of the congregation. And at midnight, he met with them in the synagogue. "Long ago," he told them, "the Jews of a Persian city were endangered by an evil vizier, whose name was Haman. But Mordecai and Esther defeated him with the help of Heaven.

"We, too, are Persian Jews in grave danger, just as in the time of Mordecai. We know that if the city falls into the hands of the rebels, they will destroy every one of us. Therefore we must put our faith in Heaven, and Heaven has revealed to me that if there is one among us willing to sacrifice his life, then we will be saved."

Now there was a very old rabbi among them who said, "I know that my days are numbered, and I am willing to sacrifice a few days of my life for the sake of the people."

Rabbi Or Shraga and all the elders thanked the old rabbi with all their hearts. Then Rabbi Or Shraga told him, "Before you come to the synagogue in the morning for Purim services, go and immerse yourself seven times in the waters of a *mikvah*. Once you have purified yourself, write on parchment the name of the angel that I will whisper to you, the angel who brings about victory in battle. But know that three hours after you write the angel's name, your spirit will take leave of this world and rise to the Throne of Glory."

The old man accepted this exalted mission, and the next day, when it was Purim, he purified himself, and wrote on a perfect piece of parchment the name that the rabbi had whispered into his ear. He brought it to the synagogue, where all the Jews of the city had gathered to celebrate Purim and to pray that the city be saved, and he gave it to Rabbi Or Shraga.

The rabbi led the frightened congregation in prayer, and then fastened the parchment to the right wing of a white dove. With all those in the synagogue watching and praying for a miracle, the rabbi carried the dove to a window facing east and set it free. As the dove took flight and passed over the heads of the rebels, huge tongues of fire broke out everywhere in the rebel camp. The terrified rebels fled in all directions, never to return. Thus did peace come to the city of Yezd. As for the old man who wrote down the secret name, three hours later he departed from this world and was welcomed into the World to Come.

Every year on Purim after that, the Jews of Yezd not only celebrated the victory of the ancient Persian Jews, but also their own victory, thanks to a miracle of God. So, too, did they fondly remember the old man who had made their victory possible, by giving his life in writing down that holy name.

Persia, oral tradition

ABOUT
"THE ANGEL OF DREAMS"

Purim

Purim celebrates the events described in the Biblical Book of Esther. On Purim the *megillah*, the scroll of Esther, is read in the synagogue. The story tells how Haman, the advisor to Ahasuerus, king of Persia, plotted to destroy the Jews of the land. He was stopped by Mordecai and by Esther, the queen, who took great risks and showed great courage in their efforts to save their people.

They ultimately defeated Haman, and it is their triumph that is celebrated on Purim, a joyous holiday with a carnival-like spirit. Children wear costumes and play with special noisemakers known as *graggers*, which are used to drown out Haman's name, and everyone celebrates with special foods, like *hamantashen*, a pastry made in the shape of Haman's hat.

(In present-day Israel they are called *ozney haman*, Haman's ears.) In some communities, the children write Haman's name on the soles of their shoes with chalk, and then stamp out the name. Since Purim is also dedicated to remembering the poor, there is a popular custom called *mishloah manot* in which gifts of food are delivered to the poor and to friends of the family. Sometimes these gifts are sent on special Purim plates containing verses from the Book of Esther.

Rabbi Or Shraga

From at least the ninth century, the Persian city of Yezd was a center for Jewish scholars. Rabbi Or Shraga was the leader of the Jewish community, and he maintained close contact with the Jews of the Persian city of Meshed, another great center of Jewish scholarship. This story demonstrates the close ties between Rabbi Or Shraga and the Shah who ruled the city. In many ways it is parallel to the ancient story of Purim, with Rabbi Or Shraga playing a role similar to that of Mordecai. This demonstrates how events in Jewish history seem to repeat themselves, and how Jewish folklore finds ways to point out these parallels.

THE MAGIC WINE CUP
A Passover Tale

In the days before Passover, a stranger was seen wandering through the streets of Mogador in the land of Morocco. Even though he was dressed in rags, he did not look like a beggar, and from the fringes on the garment he was wearing it was clear that he was a Jew.

Some of Rabbi Hayim Pinto's students wondered about this man when they saw him in the city market. And when they returned to the yeshivah, they told the rabbi about him. Rabbi Pinto had them describe the man in great detail. Then he asked them if the man had looked happy or sad. They told the rabbi that he had looked terribly sad. Indeed, just looking at his face made them sad as well.

Now, Passover is a time to remember the poor, and it was Rabbi Pinto's custom to invite the poor Jews of the city to his Seder. So on the eve of Passover he sent his students into the city to bring back all the poor Jews they could find. He told them to search especially for the stranger they had told him about, and to be sure that he came back with them.

So the rabbi's students searched every corner of the city for the poor, who were delighted to learn that they would have a place to celebrate the first night of Passover. But when the students finally found the stranger, he was sitting alone under a barren tree, and he refused to accompany them to the rabbi's Seder. "For you it is the holiday of Passover," he said, "but for me it is a time of mourning." The students did their best to persuade him, but in the end they returned empty-handed.

Now, when they told Rabbi Pinto that the man had refused their invitation, the rabbi said, "If you can't convince him to come here, whisper this word in his ear"— and he whispered it to each of his students. So the students returned to the stranger, still sitting under the tree, and they tried once more to invite him to join the rabbi's Seder. Again he refused, but this time one of the students whispered the rabbi's word into the man's ear. And as soon as he heard it, the man's eyes opened wide. He stood up and agreed to accompany them at once.

When that Jew arrived at the rabbi's house, he was greeted warmly by Rabbi Pinto. The man returned the rabbi's greetings, and then he asked, "How is it, Rabbi, that you knew the name of the ship that brought about my misfortune?"

"Join our Seder," Rabbi Pinto replied, "and you will understand how it became known to me. For now, please make yourself at home. I will have a bath prepared for you, and my students will give you fresh clothing."

The man thanked the rabbi, but he was still curious about how he had known his secret.

That night, when everyone was seated at the Seder, Rabbi Pinto introduced the guest and asked him to tell the others his story. This he did. "I was born in the city of Marrakesh," he said, "and I traveled to Spain and worked there until I had become quite wealthy. After several years, I began to miss my native land of Morocco, and thought about returning there to raise a family. With all that I had saved, I bought precious jewels.

"There was a widow whom I befriended. When she learned I was planning to return to Morocco, where her daughter lives, she asked me to bring her daughter her rightful inheritance, jewels that had belonged to her father. I agreed to do so, and I carried everything in a wooden case. But when a storm sank the ship in which I was traveling, the case was lost at sea. Somehow I managed to grab a plank and reached the shores of this city a few weeks ago. I know that I am fortunate to be alive, but after all these years, I have nothing. Even so, that is not what grieves me the most. Above all, I am heartbroken that I cannot fulfill my mission for the widow."

Now, when all those seated at the Seder heard this story, their hearts went out to the poor man who had suffered such a misfortune. Among them, there was one beautiful young woman who had tears flowing down her face. And when the man saw her grief, he, too, broke down and wept.

Rabbi Pinto said, "Do not grieve as we celebrate the Seder, but watch closely." He pointed to the Kiddush cup, which was filled with wine, and pronounced a spell over it. That spell called forth Rahab, the Angel of the Sea.

Just then everyone at the table heard a deep voice say, "Yes, Rabbi Pinto, what is your command?" They trembled with fear, for they could not see where the voice was coming from.

Then the rabbi said, "I call upon you, Rahab, Prince of the Sea, for help in finding what has been lost."

Suddenly, to everyone's amazement, the Kiddush cup began to grow larger and larger, and the wine in it was transformed into the waves of the sea. One after another the waves rose and fell, and eventually they cast up a small wooden case, which floated on the surface. The guest could hardly contain himself. "Master, that is my case!" he cried.

"Take it out!" said Rabbi Pinto. So the man reached into the enormous cup, took out the wooden case and set it on the table. At that instant the cup returned to its original size, and the waters in it became wine once more.

As everyone watched in awe, the man opened the case and saw that nothing was missing. He shed tears of joy. Then Rabbi Pinto said to him, "Now, let me introduce you to the widow's daughter to whom you were delivering the jewels." At that, the young woman who had wept at hearing the man's tale stood up with a radiant smile, and the man almost fainted with surprise. When he had regained his composure, he picked up the wooden case and placed it in her hands, much to the delight of everyone present. Then Rabbi Pinto smiled and said, "Know that nothing happens by accident. All is foretold by the Holy One, blessed be He, as is your meeting here today, for now I can tell you that I heard a heavenly voice announce that you two are destined to wed."

So it was that everyone celebrated that Seder with great happiness, and not long

after, the blessed couple was wed. From then on, every Passover, when they filled the Kiddush cup, they told the story of Rabbi Pinto and the magic wine cup that had changed their lives.

Syria, oral tradition

"THE MAGIC WINE CUP"

Passover

Passover recalls the liberation of the Israelites from slavery more than three thousand years ago. The Israelites were slaves in Egypt when God commanded Moses to tell the Egyptian Pharaoh to let the people go. When Pharaoh refused, God sent ten plagues. The tenth and most terrible plague killed every firstborn Egyptian male child. The Israelites, who had marked the doorposts of their homes with the blood of a lamb, were spared from this plague when the Angel of Death *passed over* their homes. The name Passover comes from this event. Because the Jews were slaves in Egypt, it is the custom to offer aid to the poor at this time, and to invite the hungry to share in the Seder.

Passover recalls as well the miracle of the parting of the Red Sea (also known as the Sea of Reeds), which permitted the Israelites to escape from the Egyptian army. The festival of Passover begins on the fifteenth day of the Hebrew month of Nisan (in March or April) and lasts for eight days. The highlight of the holiday is the Seder, a family meal with many symbolic foods, held on the first two nights. The Haggadah, a guidebook to the Seder, is read to recall the Exodus from Egypt. During Passover, Jews eat unleavened bread called matzah, to remind them of the unleavened bread that the Israelites made in the wilderness, when there was not time to let their dough rise. Above all, Passover represents the struggle of the Jewish people to be free of any kind of bondage.

Rabbi Hayim Pinto

Rabbi Hayim Pinto (who lived in the first half of the nineteenth century) is one of the most famous of the Moroccan rabbis. He lived in the city of Mogador most of his life. He belonged to an illustrious family, which included his father, son, and grandson all renowned for Torah study. He died at a ripe old age in 1845. His descendants now live in Ashdod, Israel.

During his lifetime, he was known for his vast knowledge and the miracles he is said to have accomplished. In this story, Rabbi Hayim Pinto shows himself to be a great kabbalistic conjurer.

THE DREAM OF THE RABBI'S DAUGHTER
A Lag ba-Omer Tale

Safed is a city in the north of Israel that has been the home of many mystics, where many a miracle has been known to take place. This is one such story.

There once was a young girl named Zohara, who had a great love of learning. Her father, Rabbi Gedalya, had named her after his favorite book, the Zohar, the most important book of Jewish mysticism. He taught her how to read Hebrew so she could join in the prayers with her mother. But he did not teach her Aramaic, the language in which the Zohar was written.

In those days it was the custom in Safed for all the leading rabbis to go to the village of Meron on the holiday of Lag ba-Omer to pray at the tomb of Rabbi Shimon bar Yohai. The families of the rabbis sometimes accompanied them to Meron, and there they set up tents outside the tomb. So it was that Zohara accompanied her father on the journey.

Now, there are two entrances to the shrine built around the tomb, one for men and the other for women, each entrance leading to a different chamber. On the men's side, the rabbis sat in a circle and passed around the mystical book of the Zohar, which Rabbi Shimon bar Yohai was said to have written. Each of the rabbis read a passage from the book; then they discussed its meaning.

Meanwhile, Zohara was on the women's side, where the women were quietly praying. She could hear all that the rabbis said in the other part of the shrine, although she could not see them. She stayed there for a long time, even after the other women finished praying and returned to their tents. She tried to follow the rabbis' discussion, but she could not, since the Zohar was written in Aramaic.

As Zohara struggled to understand the words of the rabbis, she became very sad and began to weep. She wanted so much to understand what they were saying! She wept a long time, until she became so tired that she fell asleep.

While Zohara slept, she dreamed that she was in a cave lit by a bonfire, where a rabbi with a long, white beard was teaching a class. In the dream Zohara looked around and recognized all of the greatest sages of Safed, including her father, who was sitting next to her, listening closely as the teacher spoke.

Finally the old teacher asked his students a question, but none of them knew the answer. All at once, he looked right at Zohara and asked her if she knew. Zohara was very surprised that he had called on her, and she remained silent, for she was ashamed that she did not even understand the question, much less know the answer. Then the old rabbi told her to stand up, and when she did, he blessed her with a great blessing and said, "Know that your soul is a precious one, Zohara, a soul that has come down from the highest Heaven. Know, too, that when your father named you Zohara, he bound us together. You will never have to be sad again because you do not understand. After this, whenever anyone repeats the words of the Zohar, I will come to you, and you will understand better than the best."

That is when Zohara woke up. From where she sat, she could still hear the rabbis on the other side of the wall discussing the Zohar. But this time, Zohara was astonished to discover that she understood everything they said. Then the rabbis reached such a difficult passage that none of them knew what it meant. They tried to interpret it for a long time, but at last they gave up and returned to their tents.

Zohara also left the shrine and returned to her family's tent. She told her father that she had overheard their discussion. When she repeated the difficult passage word for word, her father was amazed. "How is it possible that you can repeat these words, when you cannot even understand the language in which they are written?" he said.

Zohara then proceeded to tell her father exactly what the words meant and to explain the problem that had baffled the rabbis. Hearing his young daughter speak with such remarkable wisdom, he was filled with wonder.

Zohara told him of her dream, and of how the old rabbi had blessed her, and how he had promised to come to her whenever she heard the words of the Zohar. Her father was astounded. "I know who that old rabbi must have been," he told her.

"Please, father, who was he?" she asked.

"Surely," said Rabbi Gedalya, "he was none other than Rabbi Shimon bar Yohai himself, who came to you on Lag ba-Omer, the day in which we recall his life and death. For know that Shimon bar Yohai lived in a cave for thirteen years, and that we light campfires on Lag ba-Omer in his honor. That must be the meaning of the cave in your dream, and of the bonfire you saw burning there. Surely this means that Shimon bar Yohai has chosen to speak through you."

Rabbi Gedalya told the other rabbis about his daughter's dream and how the wisdom of Shimon bar Yohai fell from her lips. They found it hard to believe that such a miracle had taken place, and they asked if they could see for themselves.

So the rabbis of Safed came to Rabbi Gedalya's home and questioned Zohara about the most difficult passages in the Zohar. Every time she replied without hesitation, with answers so clear the rabbis felt foolish for not having understood in the first place.

Every time Zohara heard the words of the Zohar, the rabbi's spirit returned to her, revealing any mystery she wanted to know. Forever after, the rabbis of Safed treated Zohara with the greatest respect and sought her help in understanding the Zohar, for they knew that she spoke with the wisdom of Shimon bar Yohai.

Israel, oral tradition

ABOUT
"THE DREAM OF THE RABBI'S DAUGHTER"

Lag ba-Omer

In the days of Rabbi Akiba, who lived in the first century C.E., there was a terrible plague that killed many thousands of his students. The day that the plague finally ended, the eighteenth day of Iyyar (in May), was declared a holiday, known as Lag ba-Omer, which means the thirty-third day of counting the Omer. The Omer is a sheaf of barley from the new grain harvest that was brought to the Holy Temple as an offering on the second day of Passover. The Torah commands the people to count seven weeks from the time of offering the Omer ending on the holiday of Shavuot.

In later times, Lag ba-Omer also became linked with the day manna first began to fall, which is described in chapter 16 of Exodus. But at present this holiday is more strongly associated with Rabbi Shimon bar Yohai, who was said to have spent thirteen years hiding in a cave from the Romans, finally emerging on the day of Lag ba-Omer.

Lag ba-Omer is a popular holiday in modern Israel, in which campfires are lit all over the country, but especially in the Galilee, in honor of Shimon bar Yohai. Huge crowds gather at his tomb for a joyous celebration, and scores of weddings are held, adding to the festive atmosphere. Lag ba-Omer is also a day on which the book of the Zohar is studied, as in this tale.

Rabbi Shimon bar Yohai

Rabbi Shimon bar Yohai, one of the great talmudic sages, lived in the second century C.E. He was a pupil of Rabbi Akiba. At that time the Romans had conquered Jerusalem and had forbidden the study of the Torah. Rabbi Shimon criticized the Romans privately, but a traitor reported his comments to the Romans, who condemned him to death.

So Rabbi Shimon and his son Elazar went into hiding in a cave near the city of Tiberias for thirteen years. Legend has it that a spring miraculously appeared in that cave to provide them with fresh water, and a carob tree grew outside the cave to hide them and provide them with food.

Elijah the Prophet is also said to have visited them every day and taught them secrets of Heaven. Tradition holds that Rabbi Shimon wrote down these secrets, which formed the famous book of the Zohar, the primary text of Jewish mysticism. However, modern scholars say that the Zohar was not written by Shimon bar Yohai in the second century, but by Rabbi Moshe de Leon in the thirteenth century. Shimon bar Yohai's grave is found in Meron in northern Israel, and a shrine has been built around it, exactly as described in this story.

Spirit Possession in Judaism

Jewish folklore describes two kinds of possession by spirits. The most famous kind is known as possession by a *dybbuk*. A *dybbuk* is the spirit of a dead person, usually an evil one, that enters the body of a vulnerable person and takes possession of him or her. An exorcism ceremony must be done in order to expel the evil spirit. An example of *dybbuk* possession is found in the famous play *The Dybbuk*, by S. Ansky, first performed in 1920. Here a bride is possessed by the *dybbuk* on the day of her wedding, and the final act of the play presents an authentic rabbinic exorcism ceremony.

There is another kind of possession in Jewish tradition, a positive kind. This is known as possession by *ibbur* (literally, "impregnation.") An *ibbur* is the spirit of a dead sage who comes back to aid someone. The *ibbur* fuses with the soul of the person it is helping, instilling additional faith and wisdom. Unlike a *dybbuk*, which must be exorcised, an *ibbur* usually possesses someone only temporarily and is associated with some kind of sacred object, such as the book of the Zohar in this story.

A Gift for Jerusalem
A Shavuot Tale

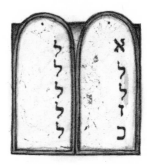

Long ago, in the hills of the Galilee, far from the city of Jerusalem, there lived a boy named Haninah ben Dosa, who was the son of a stonecutter. Haninah came from a poor family. They were so poor that they had little to eat except for the carobs and olives that grew wild.

Every year, before Shavuot, the people of Hanina's village would prepare to go up to Jerusalem for an annual pilgrimage to the Holy Temple. They would take the finest fruits of the harvest, or the finest sheep or goat from their herds, bringing them as a gift for the Temple.

Haninah would watch his neighbors as they prepared for their journey. He listened carefully as they told tales of past visits to Jerusalem; they spoke of the cool, crisp air there, of the beautiful sunsets, and of the magnificent Holy Temple, shining with gold. Haninah heard their stories and wished to go to Jerusalem more than anything. But Haninah's family was so poor that they had neither an animal nor any fruits to offer. So it was that year after year, Haninah watched his neighbors as they left for their journey, returning with tales of the golden city of Jerusalem.

Haninah would help his friends and neighbors pack and prepare for their journey. But one year, Haninah was so sad that he wouldn't be able to go that he took a walk instead. He walked through the village, his head bowed down.

Suddenly, he came across a stone. It was the biggest stone he had ever seen, and Haninah came up with a wonderful idea. He ran home, hurrying past his neighbors.

He grabbed a hammer and a chisel, and ran back to the site of the stone.

Then Haninah started to work on that stone. He chiseled and fashioned it, carving in beautiful designs. The next day, he ran back to the stone and continued his work. For three days, Haninah worked on the stone, taking breaks only for meals. Finally he polished the stone until it shone brightly in the sun.

Haninah stepped back and looked at his finished stone, smiling widely. He had carved four majestic angels. "This," he exclaimed triumphantly, "is the best thing I have ever made. It will be perfect for the Temple in Jerusalem."

Haninah ran to invite his neighbors to see his work of art. They gathered around the stone.

"Haninah, this is truly a masterpiece!" said the baker.

"Look at the detail of the wings. The angels appear so alive," said the weaver.

"Yes, as if they could jump out of the stone and fly," added the shoemaker.

"Oh," said Haninah, "then you can take it with you on your journey to Jerusalem! For if I can't go to Jerusalem, at least my gift will go." Haninah put his arms around that stone and tried to lift it, to give it to them. But the stone did not budge. He tried again. Nothing.

The neighbors looked at each other baffled. Their eyes turned downward, they replied: "Haninah, the stone is beautiful. But it is much too heavy for us to take on the long journey to Jerusalem. Maybe you can draw a picture of the angels and we could take that instead." Haninah did not utter a word. One by one, the neighbors went back to their preparations. When they had all gone, Haninah stretched out on his rock and cried.

Now God looked down from Heaven and saw Haninah's deep desire to go to Jerusalem. God saw the love and dedication he had put into creating a gift for the Temple. And God caused a miracle to take place. As Haninah's tears rolled across that stone, each tear touched one of the stone angels, and at that instant they rose up and came to life, much to Haninah's amazement.

Then, with a swift flap of their wings, the four angels lifted the stone, with Haninah on top of it, up into the air. Haninah found himself flying across the heav-

ens toward Jerusalem, along with the angels. As they approached Jerusalem, the city first appeared as a jewel glowing in the distance. Haninah laughed out loud. "Now I know why Jerusalem is called the jewel in God's crown!"

Soon Haninah was standing near the entrance of the Temple in Jerusalem, and the stone rested beside him, with the angels carved into the stone once more. Just then a group of weary pilgrims arrived, and when they saw what Haninah had carved, they said, "Look at that beautiful stone! Let us rest here." Haninah was filled with joy, for a miracle had brought his gift to Jerusalem, and now it would serve as a place for weary travelers to sit and rest.

When Haninah ben Dosa grew up, he became one of the greatest rabbis. Even to this day, people tell loving tales about him. As for the stone he had carved, it remained there as long as the Temple was still standing. But when the Temple was torn down, the stone disappeared. Some say it was used in rebuilding the walls of Jerusalem. Others say that the same angels who brought it to Jerusalem later brought it to the magical Temple in heavenly Jerusalem, where Haninah now makes his home.

Babylon, fifth century

ABOUT
"A GIFT FOR JERUSALEM"

Shavuot

Shavuot takes place on the sixth day of the Hebrew month of Sivan (in May or June). It was originally a spring harvest festival in the land of Israel, one of three yearly pilgrimage festivals in Judaism, along with Passover and Sukkot. All three festivals recall the events of the Exodus from Egypt. While Passover celebrates the departure from Egypt, and Sukkot commemorates the forty years the Israelites wandered in the desert, Shavuot celebrates the day on which the Ten Commandments and the rest of the Torah were given at Mount Sinai, establishing an eternal covenant between God and the Jewish people.

It was the custom in ancient Israel for all of the people to gather at the Temple in Jerusalem during the three pilgrimage festivals. They would bring an offering for the Temple—as Haninah does in this story—usually the best of their harvest or livestock. In this way they gave their thanks to God. Haninah's gift is an unusual one in that it does not fit into either of these categories.

In the Sephardic prayerbook, a Jewish wedding contract (a *ketubah*) is read on Shavuot, in which God is described as the bridegroom and Israel as the bride, and they swear eternal allegiance to each other. Thus celebrating Shavuot reenacts the ancient covenant of the Jewish people with God.

Rabbi Haninah ben Dosa

Haninah ben Dosa, who lived in the first century C.E., grew up to become one of the most respected and beloved of the talmudic rabbis. He lived in the Land of Israel in the town of Arav in the Galilee, where he worked as a stonecutter. Although he and his wife were extremely poor, Rabbi Hanina refused to accept charity, and often all they had to eat were carob pods.

The miracle that takes place in this story shows that God cares not about the gift itself but the intention in giving it. That is why angels appear to help Haninah carry the heavy stone all the way to Jerusalem.

It is said that Rabbi Haninah was so righteous that God showed favor to the entire generation for his sake.

Ascending to Jerusalem (Aliyah)

Jerusalem is in the hills of Israel, and those who go there are said to *ascend* to Jerusalem. The Hebrew term for this is *aliyah*, which means "ascent." This term is also used in the synagogue for those who are called upon to "ascend" to the pulpit, to participate in the reading of the Torah. Jews living outside of Israel who decide to move there are said to "go up to the Land of Israel." The modern term is to "make *aliyah*." Thus the use of the term *"aliyah"* in connection with Jerusalem shows just how holy the city is considered to be.

THE DAY THE RABBI DISAPPEARED
A Sabbath Tale

The sages of Fez had a dream: to bring the greatest living sage in the world to visit their city in the land of Morocco. It is said that for every two Jews, you will find three opinions, but in this matter all agreed: the greatest sage was none other than Moses Maimonides, known to the world as the Rambam.

At that time, the Rambam was living in Egypt. But before he had written his great books and had become the Jewish leader of the city of Cairo, he had lived in Fez for several years. Now his illustrious name was spoken of wherever Jews could be found, and the sages of Fez longed to study Torah with him again. So they sent a messenger to Cairo, inviting him to return for a visit. And before a month had passed, the messenger brought back a letter from the Rambam.

The sages were delighted to learn that the Rambam would indeed be coming to Fez. But they were mystified, too. For the Rambam had written that although he would stay in Fez for a month, he would spend each Sabbath in the city of Jerusalem. How was that possible? Jerusalem was far away, and if the Rambam spent the week in Fez, he could never reach Jerusalem by the Sabbath.

One of the sages spoke. "Perhaps the Rambam does not want us to interpret his words literally. Perhaps he means to say that on the Sabbath his heart lies in Jerusalem, so much so that it is as if he were not present among us." The others marveled at the wisdom of these words.

At last the Rambam arrived. He was greeted with joy by the entire Jewish population of Fez. Each day he met with the sages, sharing his knowledge of the Torah. But on Friday the Rambam asked to remain alone, so that he could prepare for the Sabbath. And at sunset, when the Sabbath began, the Rambam was nowhere to be seen. The people understood that he must have gone somewhere else. But where? For there was simply no way he could have reached Jerusalem.

Then, right after the Havdalah ceremony that ends the Sabbath, the Rambam rejoined the sages, and when they asked him where he had been, he said, "In Jerusalem."

This happened two more times. Every week, just before the beginning of the Sabbath, the Rambam disappeared. And no one knew where he went.

Now there were two boys in Fez who had heard tales of the Rambam's miracles. They believed him when he said he went to Jerusalem on the Sabbath, and more than anything in the world, they wanted to know how he did it. So they climbed a tree outside his house and waited and watched.

The Rambam spent all day Friday writing in his study, until a few minutes before sunset. Then he went up the stairs to the roof, wearing his Sabbath robe.

The boys could see the Rambam clearly from the tree, but he didn't seem to notice them. His gaze was turned inward. Then, just before sunset heralded the onset of the Sabbath, he pronounced a spell consisting of strange names the boys had never heard. All at once they saw something like a falling star that landed right where the Rambam was standing, and then it was gone. And they saw that the Rambam, too, had disappeared.

The boys could hardly believe their eyes, yet they had seen the miracle themselves. They decided that the Rambam must have pronounced a magic spell invoking an angel—for what else could that falling star have been?—and now surely, he was praying in Jerusalem.

And they were right.

Morocco, oral tradition

ABOUT

"THE DAY THE RABBI DISAPPEARED"

The Sabbath

The Book of Genesis tells how God created the world in six days and rested on the seventh, making it a holy day, the Sabbath. Every week Jews observe the Sabbath as a day of joy and rest. The famous Jewish philosopher Ahad Ha'am once said, "More than Israel has kept the Sabbath, the Sabbath has kept Israel." This means that the existence of the Sabbath has given a special rhythm and meaning to Jewish life. The commandment to keep the Sabbath is the fourth of the ten commandments: *Remember the Sabbath day to keep it holy. Six days you shall labor and do all your work, but the seventh day is a sabbath of God: you shall not do any work* (Exodus 20:8–10).

The Sabbath is very much a family holiday and a time to appreciate things at a leisurely pace. Sabbath rituals include Friday evening services, where a special prayer, *Lekhah Dodi,* is sung to welcome the Sabbath Queen. At home there is the lighting of the Sabbath candles and a family Sabbath meal, with blessings over wine and bread. There is an ancient tradition that every Jew receives a second soul during the Sabbath, known as a *neshamah yetayrah.* A special ceremony for the end of the Sabbath, known as Havdalah, includes the smelling of fragrant spices that symbolize reluctance to see the Sabbath end—and one's second soul depart.

The Rambam

Rabbi Moses ben Maimon (1135–1204) is known both as Maimonides and by the Hebrew acronym Rambam. As the greatest Jewish philosopher, he is so highly regarded that the inscription on his tombstone reads, "From Moses [in the Bible] to Moses [Maimonides], there was none like Moses." The Rambam lived most of his life in Egypt, where he was the court physician as well as the leader of the Jewish community. He did, however, live in the city of Fez for several years, as reported in this tale, which was collected in modern Israel from a Jew from the city of Fez.

Among the Rambam's most famous books are the *Mishneh Torah,* a commentary on the Mishnah, and *The Guide to the Perplexed.* The Rambam defined the "Thirteen Principles of Faith," which became the essential list of Jewish beliefs. Although he himself disputed the existence of magic, there are many legends about him found throughout the Middle East in which he plays the role of a sorcerer, as in this tale.

GLOSSARY

etrog (EH-troge) A citrus fruit, the citron, that is carried and shaken with the *lulav* during the Sukkot synagogue service.

Gan Eden (GAHN AY-den) The Garden of Eden.

gragger (GRAH-ger) Noisemaker used to celebrate Purim.

hamantashen (HAH-mun-tah-shun) Three-cornered pastries served on Purim, said to have been modeled on Haman's hat.

hanukkiyah (hah-nu-key-YAH) A special eight-branched menorah with a *shammash*, a helper candle, used during the eight days of Hanukkah.

Hasidism (ha-SEED-ism or ha-seed-IS-um) A movement of spiritual revival in Judaism founded by the Baal Shem Tov in the eighteenth century. It emphasizes ways of becoming closer to God through prayer, dancing, singing, and storytelling.

hazan (hah-ZAHN or HAH-zun) A cantor.

Hoshanah Rabbah (ho-SHAH-nah RAH-bah) The seventh and final day of Sukkot, on which it is customary to stay up studying all night. Legend holds that the heavens open for an instant at midnight, and any wish made at that time comes true.

Kabbalah (literally "to receive"; kah-bah-LA or kah-BAH-la) The Jewish mystical tradition and its literature.

Kiddush cup (key-DOOSH or KID-dish) A goblet used when blessings are said over wine on the Sabbath and other holidays.

lulav (loo-LAHV or LOO-lahv) A palm branch, tied together with sprigs of willow and myrtle, carried and shaken during the Sukkot synagogue service.

Megillah (literally "scroll"; meh-gi-LA or meh-GIL-la) Usually refers to the Book of Esther.

menorah (meh-no-RA or men-NO-ra) The seven-branched candelabrum described in the Bible and used in Temple days.

mikvah (MIK-vah) The pool used for ritual purification, primarily by women.

minyan (min-YAHN or MIN-yahn) A prayer service traditionally requires a minimum of ten men in order to take place. These ten men are known as a *minyan*. Many congregations now count women in the *minyan* as well.

Rabbi A teacher of Judaism who is qualified to decide matters of Jewish law.

Seder (SAY-der) A ritual meal that takes place during Passover.

shalom aleichem (literally "Peace unto you"; sha-LOME ah-LAY-hem) The traditional Jewish greeting. The reply is *Aleichem shalom,* meaning "Unto you, peace."

shofar (sho-FAR or SHO-fur) A ram's horn, used as a wind instrument.

Talmud (tal-MOOD or TAL-mud) The second most sacred Jewish text, after the Torah. The Talmud was codified around the fifth century C.E.

Tetragrammaton (te-truh-GRA-muh-ton) A Greek word for the four-letter name of God, whose true pronunciation is a great secret. Jews substitute *Adonai* or *Ha-Shem* when they reach this word in their prayers.

Torah (toe-RAH or TOE-rah) The first five books of the Bible, which God is said to have dictated to Moses at Mount Sinai. The most sacred Jewish text of all.

yeshivah (yuh-SHE-vah) A school for Jewish students, in which they are taught primarily Torah and Talmud.

Zohar (ZO-har) The central work of Jewish mysticism, traditionally attributed to Rabbi Shimon bar Yohai of the second century C.E. but now considered to have been written in the thirteenth century by Rabbi Moshe de Leon and his disciples.

SOURCES
All sources are in Hebrew unless otherwise noted.

A Flock of Angels (**Kurdistan**) From *Kehillot Yehudei Kurdistan*, edited by Abraham Ben-Jacob (Jerusalem, 1961). A variant is IFA (Israel Folktale Archives) 11165, collected by Avraham Keren from Yitzak Izador Firestein of Poland.

Drawing the Wind (**The Balkans**) This story was collected during World War I by the folklorist Max Grunwald from an unknown Jewish teller from the Balkans. It was published in *Sippurei-am, Romanssot, ve-Orehot-hayim shel Yehude Sefarad* by Max Grunwald, edited by Dov Noy (Jerusalem, 1982). There are many variants of this tale told among Sephardic communities. The Israel Folktale Archives has collected more than one hundred versions. In some versions the imprisoned rabbi is identified as Rabbi Ephraim ben Yisrael Ankawa of Tlemcen, Tunisia.

The Cottage of Candles (**Afghanistan**) IFA 7830, collected by Zevulon Qort from Ben Zion Asherov, published in *Sippurei-am Mipi Yehudei Afghanistan* (Tel Aviv, 1983). A variant is found in *Ha-Na'al ha-Ktanah*, edited by Asher Barash (Tel Aviv, 1966). Another variant, in which there are bottles of oil in a cave, and a person lives until the oil is exhausted is IFA 8335, collected by Moshe Rabi from Hannah Haddad, in *Avotenu Sipru* (Jerusalem, 1976). "Godfather Death" is a variant of this story found in *Grimm's Fairy Tales.*

Four Who Entered Paradise (**Morocco**) IFA 13901, collected by Yaakov Alfasi of Morocco from Rabbi Shimon Elkayam of Azmor, Morocco. This tale is clearly based on the famous tale about four sages who entered Paradise found in the Babylonian Talmud (Haggigah 14b). Traditions about Hoshanah Rabbah are from IFA 1257, collected by Zevulun Qort from Zohara Bezalel of Afghanistan. A variant about the sky opening (this time on Shavuot) is IFA 4014, collected by Pinhas Gutterman from Rabbi Shalom Weinstein of Poland.

The Flying Shoe (**Eastern Europe**) From *Gan ha-Hasidut*, edited by Eliezer Steinmann (Jerusalem, 1957).

The Enchanted Menorah (**Germany**) From *Me-Otsar Genazai* by Hayim Dov Armon Kastenbaum, edited by Alter Ze'ev Wortheim (Tel Aviv, 1932). From Hayim Dov Armon Kastenbaum, who heard this story from his grandmother.

The Souls of Trees (**Eastern Europe**) From *Sihot Moharan* in *Hayye Moharan* by Rabbi Nathan of Bratslav (Lemberg, West Ukraine, 1874). Rabbi Nathan was Rabbi Nachman's scribe, and wrote down all his teachings. The passage Rabbi Nachman's finger lands on is from the Talmud (B. Baba Kama 92b and B. Sukkah 29a).

The Angel of Dreams (**Persia**) IFA 1375. Collected by Hanina Mizrahi from Yaakov Yazdi.

The Magic Wine Cup (**Syria**) IFA 6628, collected by Moshe Rabi from Avraham Etia, in *Avotenu Sipru*, edited by Moshe Rabi (Jerusalem, 1976), story no. 47.

The Dream of the Rabbi's Daughter (**Israel**) IFA 612, collected by S. Arnest.

A Gift for Jerusalem (**Babylon**) From the Babylonian Talmud (Taanit 25a). An oral variant is IFA 399 from Poland.

The Day the Rabbi Disappeared (**Morocco**) IFA 15512. Collected by Yifrach Haviv from Yoram Harush of Fez, Morocco.

The Adventures of Paddington

THE
ADVENTURES OF
PADDINGTON

CONTAINING *A Bear Called Paddington*
AND *More About Paddington*

by MICHAEL BOND

with DRAWINGS AND COLOUR PLATES
by PEGGY FORTNUM

COLLINS
St James's Place
London

ISBN 0 00 182150 4

© *this edition Michael Bond, 1965*
First Impression January 1976
Second Impression August 1976
Printed in Great Britain
Collins Clear-Type Press
London and Glasgow

A Bear Called Paddington

CONTENTS

CHAPTER ONE

Please Look After this Bear

MR. AND MRS. Brown first met Paddington on a
railway platform. In fact, that was how he came to
have such an unusual name for a bear, for Paddington
was the name of the station.

The Browns were there to meet their daughter
Judy, who was coming home from school for the
holidays. It was a warm summer day and the station
was crowded with people on their way to the seaside.
Trains were whistling, taxis hooting, porters rushing

7

about shouting at one another, and altogether there was so much noise that Mr. Brown, who saw him first, had to tell his wife several times before she understood.

" A *bear*? On Paddington station? " Mrs. Brown looked at her husband in amazement. " Don't be silly, Henry. There can't be! "

Mr. Brown adjusted his glasses. " But there is," he insisted. " I distinctly saw it. Over there—behind those mailbags. It was wearing a funny kind of hat."

Without waiting for a reply he caught hold of his wife's arm and pushed her through the crowd, round a trolley laden with chocolate and cups of tea, past a bookstall, and through a gap in a pile of suitcases towards the Lost Property Office.

" There you are," he announced, triumphantly, pointing towards a dark corner. " I told you so! "

Mrs. Brown followed the direction of his arm and dimly made out a small, furry object in the shadows. It seemed to be sitting on some kind of suitcase and around its neck there was a label with some writing on it. The suitcase was old and battered and on the side, in large letters, were the words WANTED ON VOYAGE.

Mrs. Brown clutched at her husband. " Why, Henry," she exclaimed. " I believe you were right after all. It *is* a bear! "

She peered at it more closely. It seemed a very

unusual kind of bear. It was brown in colour, a rather dirty brown, and it was wearing a most odd-looking hat, with a wide brim, just as Mr. Brown had said. From beneath the brim two large, round eyes stared back at her.

Seeing that something was expected of it the bear stood up and politely raised its hat, revealing two black ears. " Good afternoon," it said, in a small, clear voice.

" Er . . . good afternoon," replied Mr. Brown, doubtfully. There was a moment of silence.

The bear looked at them inquiringly. " Can I help you? "

Mr. Brown looked rather embarrassed. " Well . . . no. Er . . . as a matter of fact, we were wondering if we could help you."

Mrs. Brown bent down. " You're a very small bear," she said.

The bear puffed out its chest. " I'm a very rare sort of bear," he replied, importantly. " There aren't many of us left where I come from."

" And where is that? " asked Mrs. Brown.

The bear looked round carefully before replying. " Darkest Peru. I'm not really supposed to be here at all. I'm a stowaway! "

" A stowaway? " Mr. Brown lowered his voice and looked anxiously over his shoulder. He almost expected to see a policeman standing behind him with a notebook and pencil, taking everything down.

9

"Yes," said the bear. "I emigrated, you know." A sad expression came into its eyes. "I used to live with my Aunt Lucy in Peru, but she had to go into a home for retired bears."

"You don't mean to say you've come all the way from South America by yourself?" exclaimed Mrs. Brown.

The bear nodded. "Aunt Lucy always said she wanted me to emigrate when I was old enough. That's why she taught me to speak English."

"But whatever did you do for food?" asked Mr. Brown. "You must be starving."

Bending down, the bear unlocked the suitcase with a small key, which it also had round its neck, and brought out an almost empty glass jar. "I ate marmalade," he said, rather proudly. "Bears like marmalade. And I lived in a lifeboat."

"But what are you going to do now?" said Mr. Brown. "You can't just sit on Paddington station waiting for something to happen."

"Oh, I shall be all right . . . I expect." The bear bent down to do up its case again. As he did so Mrs. Brown caught a glimpse of the writing on the label. It said, simply, PLEASE LOOK AFTER THIS BEAR. THANK YOU.

She turned appealingly to her husband. "Oh, Henry, what *shall* we do? We can't just leave him here. There's no knowing what might happen to him. London's such a big place when you've nowhere to

10

go. Can't he come and stay with us for a few days?"

Mr. Brown hesitated. "But Mary, dear, we can't take him . . . not just like that. After all . . ."

"After all, *what*?" Mrs. Brown's voice had a firm note to it. She looked down at the bear. "He *is* rather sweet. And he'd be such company for Jonathan and Judy. Even if it's only for a little while. They'd never forgive you if they knew you'd left him here."

"It all seems highly irregular," said Mr. Brown, doubtfully. "I'm sure there's a law about it." He bent down. "Would you like to come and stay with us?" he asked. "That is," he added, hastily, not wishing to offend the bear, "if you've nothing else planned."

The bear jumped and his hat nearly fell off with excitement. "Oooh, yes, please. I should like that very much. I've nowhere to go and everyone seems in such a hurry."

"Well, that's settled then," said Mrs. Brown, before her husband could change his mind. "And you can have marmalade for breakfast every morning, and——" she tried hard to think of something else that bears might like.

"*Every* morning?" The bear looked as if it could hardly believe its ears. "I only had it on special occasions at home. Marmalade's very expensive in Darkest Peru."

"Then you shall have it every morning starting

11

to-morrow," continued Mrs. Brown. "And honey on Sunday."

A worried expression came over the bear's face. "Will it cost very much?" he asked. "You see, I haven't very much money."

"Of course not. We wouldn't dream of charging you anything. We shall expect you to be one of the family, shan't we, Henry?" Mrs. Brown looked at her husband for support.

"Of course," said Mr. Brown. "By the way," he added, "if you *are* coming home with us you'd better know our names. This is Mrs. Brown and I'm Mr. Brown."

The bear raised its hat politely—twice. "I haven't really got a name," he said. "Only a Peruvian one which no one can understand."

"Then we'd better give you an English one," said Mrs. Brown. "It'll make things much easier." She looked round the station for inspiration. "It ought to be something special," she said thoughtfully. As she spoke an engine standing in one of the platforms gave a loud whistle and let off a cloud of steam. "I know what!" she exclaimed. "We found you on Paddington station so we'll call you Paddington!"

"Paddington!" The bear repeated it several times to make sure. "It seems a very long name."

"Quite distinguished," said Mr. Brown. "Yes, I like Paddington as a name. Paddington it shall be."

Mrs. Brown stood up. " Good. Now, Paddington, I have to meet our little daughter, Judy, off the train. She's coming home from school. I'm sure you must be thirsty after your long journey, so you go along to the buffet with Mr. Brown and he'll buy you a nice cup of tea."

Paddington licked his lips. " I'm *very* thirsty," he said. " Sea water makes you thirsty." He picked up his suitcase, pulled his hat down firmly over his head, and waved a paw politely in the direction of the buffet. " After you, Mr. Brown."

" Er . . . thank you, Paddington," said Mr. Brown.

" Now, Henry, look after him," Mrs. Brown called after them. " And for goodness' sake, when you get a moment, take that label off his neck. It makes him look like a parcel. I'm sure he'll get put in a luggage van or something if a porter sees him."

The buffet was crowded when they entered but Mr. Brown managed to find a table for two in a corner. By standing on a chair Paddington could just rest his paws comfortably on the glass top. He looked around with interest while Mr. Brown went to fetch the tea. The sight of everyone eating reminded him of how hungry he felt. There was a half-eaten bun on the table but just as he reached out his paw a waitress came up and swept it into a pan.

" You don't want that, dearie," she said, giving him a friendly pat. " You don't know where it's been."

Paddington felt so empty he didn't really mind

13

where it had been but he was much too polite to say anything.

" Well, Paddington," said Mr. Brown, as he placed two steaming cups of tea on the table and a plate piled high with cakes. " How's that to be going on with ? "

Paddington's eyes glistened. " It's very nice, thank you," he exclaimed, eyeing the tea doubtfully. " But it's rather hard drinking out of a cup. I usually get my head stuck, or else my hat falls in and makes it taste nasty."

Mr. Brown hesitated. " Then you'd better give your hat to me. I'll pour the tea into a saucer for you. It's not really done in the best circles, but I'm sure no one will mind just this once."

Paddington removed his hat and laid it carefully on the table while Mr. Brown poured out the tea. He looked hungrily at the cakes, in particular at a large cream-and-jam one which Mr. Brown placed on a plate in front of him.

" There you are, Paddington," he said. " I'm sorry they haven't any marmalade ones, but they were the best I could get."

" I'm glad I emigrated," said Paddington, as he reached out a paw and pulled the plate nearer. " Do you think anyone would mind if I stood on the table to eat ? "

Before Mr. Brown could answer he had climbed up and placed his right paw firmly on the bun. It was a

very large bun, the biggest and stickiest Mr. Brown
had been able to find, and in a matter of moments
most of the inside found its way on to Paddington's
whiskers. People started to nudge each other and

began staring in their direction. Mr. Brown wished
he had chosen a plain, ordinary bun, but he wasn't
very experienced in the ways of bears. He stirred his
tea and looked out of the window, pretending he had
tea with a bear on Paddington station every day of
his life.

"Henry!" The sound of his wife's voice brought
him back to earth with a start. "Henry, whatever

are you doing to that poor bear? Look at him! He's covered all over with cream and jam."

Mr. Brown jumped up in confusion. "He seemed rather hungry," he answered, lamely.

Mrs. Brown turned to her daughter. "This is what happens when I leave your father alone for five minutes."

Judy clapped her hands excitedly. "Oh, Daddy, is he really going to stay with us?"

"If he does," said Mrs. Brown, "I can see someone other than your father will have to look after him. Just look at the mess he's in!"

Paddington, who all this time had been too interested in his bun to worry about what was going on, suddenly became aware that people were talking about him. He looked up to see that Mrs. Brown had been joined by a little girl, with laughing blue eyes and long, fair hair. He jumped up, meaning to raise his hat, and in his haste slipped on a patch of strawberry jam which somehow or other had found its way on to the glass table-top. For a brief moment he had a dizzy impression of everything and everyone being upside down. He waved his paws wildly in the air and then, before anyone could catch him, he somersaulted backwards and landed with a splash in his saucer of tea. He jumped up even quicker than he had sat down, because the tea was still very hot, and promptly stepped into Mr. Brown's cup.

Judy threw back her head and laughed until the

tears rolled down her face. " Oh, Mummy, isn't he
funny! " she cried.

Paddington, who didn't think it at all funny, stood
for a moment with one foot on the table and the other
in Mr. Brown's tea. There were large patches of
white cream all over his face, and on his left ear there
was a lump of strawberry jam.

" You wouldn't think," said Mrs. Brown, " that
anyone could get in such a state with just one
bun."

Mr. Brown coughed. He had just caught the stern
eye of a waitress on the other side of the counter.
" Perhaps," he said, " we'd better go. I'll see if I

can find a taxi." He picked up Judy's belongings and hurried outside.

Paddington stepped gingerly off the table and, with a last look at the sticky remains of his bun, climbed down on to the floor.

Judy took one of his paws. "Come along, Paddington. We'll take you home and you can have a nice hot bath. Then you can tell me all about South America. I'm sure you must have had lots of wonderful adventures."

"I have," said Paddington, earnestly. "Lots. Things are always happening to me. I'm that sort of bear."

When they came out of the buffet Mr. Brown had already found a taxi and he waved them across. The driver looked hard at Paddington and then at the inside of his nice, clean taxi.

"Bears is sixpence extra," he said, gruffly. "Sticky bears is ninepence!"

"He can't help being sticky, driver," said Mr. Brown. "He's just had a nasty accident."

The driver hesitated. "All right, 'op in. But mind none of it comes off on me interior. I only cleaned it out this morning."

The Browns trooped obediently into the back of the taxi. Mr. and Mrs. Brown and Judy sat in the back, while Paddington stood on a tip-up seat behind the driver so that he could see out of the window.

The sun was shining as they drove out of the station and after the gloom and the noise everything seemed bright and cheerful. They swept past a group of people at a bus stop and Paddington waved. Several people stared and one man raised his hat in return. It was all very friendly. After weeks of sitting alone in a lifeboat there was so much to see. There were people and cars and big, red buses everywhere—it wasn't a bit like Darkest Peru.

Paddington kept one eye out of the window in case he missed anything. With his other eye he carefully examined Mr. and Mrs. Brown and Judy. Mr. Brown was fat and jolly, with a big moustache and glasses, while Mrs. Brown, who was also rather plump, looked like a larger edition of Judy. Paddington had just decided he was going to like staying with the Browns when the glass window behind the driver shot back and a gruff voice said, " Where did you say you wanted to go? "

Mr. Brown leaned forward. " Number thirty-two, Windsor Gardens."

The driver cupped his ear with one hand. " Can't 'ear you," he shouted.

Paddington tapped him on the shoulder. " Number thirty-two, Windsor Gardens," he repeated.

The taxi driver jumped at the sound of Paddington's voice and narrowly missed hitting a bus. He looked down at his shoulder and glared. " Cream! " he said, bitterly. " All over me new coat! "

Judy giggled and Mr. and Mrs. Brown exchanged glances. Mr. Brown peered at the meter. He half expected to see a sign go up saying they had to pay another sixpence.

" I beg your pardon," said Paddington. He bent forward and tried to rub the stain off with his other paw. Several bun crumbs and a smear of jam added themselves mysteriously to the taxi driver's coat. The driver gave Paddington a long, hard look. Paddington raised his hat and the driver slammed the window shut again.

" Oh dear," said Mrs. Brown. " We really shall have to give him a bath as soon as we get indoors. It's getting everywhere."

Paddington looked thoughtful. It wasn't so much that he didn't like baths; he really didn't mind being covered with jam and cream. It seemed a pity to wash it all off quite so soon. But before he had time to consider the matter the taxi stopped and the Browns began to climb out. Paddington picked up his suitcase and followed Judy up a flight of white steps to a big green door.

" Now you're going to meet Mrs. Bird," said Judy. " She looks after us. She's a bit fierce sometimes and she grumbles a lot but she doesn't really mean it. I'm sure you'll like her."

Paddington felt his knees begin to tremble. He looked round for Mr. and Mrs. Brown, but they appeared to be having some sort of argument with the

taxi driver. Behind the door he could hear footsteps approaching.

"I'm sure I shall like her, if you say so," he said, catching sight of his reflection on the brightly polished letter-box. "But will she like me?"

CHAPTER TWO

A Bear in Hot Water

PADDINGTON WASN'T quite sure what to expect when Mrs. Bird opened the door. He was pleasantly surprised when they were greeted by a stout, motherly lady with grey hair and a kindly twinkle in her eyes. When she saw Judy she raised her hands above her head. "Goodness gracious, you've arrived already," she said, in horror. "And me hardly finished the washing up. I suppose you'll be wanting tea?"

"Hallo, Mrs. Bird," said Judy. "It's nice to see you again. How's the rheumatism?"

"Worse than it's ever been," began Mrs. Bird—

then she stopped speaking and stared at Paddington. "Whatever have you got there?" she asked. "What is it?"

"It's not a *what*," said Judy. "It's a bear. His name's Paddington."

Paddington raised his hat.

"A *bear*," said Mrs. Bird, doubtfully. "Well, he has good manners, I'll say that for him."

"He's going to stay with us," announced Judy. "He's emigrated from South America and he's all alone with nowhere to go."

"Going to *stay* with us?" Mrs. Bird raised her arms again. "How long for?"

Judy looked round mysteriously before replying. "I don't know," she said. "It depends on *things*."

"Mercy me," exclaimed Mrs. Bird. "I wish you'd told me. I haven't put clean sheets in the spare room or anything." She looked down at Paddington. "Though judging by the state he's in perhaps that's as well!"

"It's all right, Mrs. Bird," said Paddington. "I think I'm going to have a bath. I had an accident with a bun."

"Oh!" Mrs. Bird held the door open. "Oh, well in that case you'd best come on in. Only mind the carpet. It's just been done."

Judy took hold of Paddington's paw and squeezed. "She doesn't mind really," she whispered. "I think she rather likes you."

23

Paddington watched the retreating figure of Mrs. Bird. " She seems a bit fierce," he said.

Mrs. Bird turned. " What was that you said? "

Paddington jumped. " I . . . I . . ." he began.

" Where was it you said you'd come from? Peru? "

" That's right," said Paddington. " Darkest Peru."

" Humph! " Mrs. Bird looked thoughtful for a moment. " Then I expect you like marmalade. I'd better get some more from the grocer."

" There you are! What did I tell you? " cried Judy, as the door shut behind Mrs. Bird. " She *does* like you."

" Fancy her knowing I like marmalade," said Paddington.

" Mrs. Bird knows everything about everything," said Judy. " Now, you'd better come upstairs with me and I'll show you your room. It used to be mine when I was small and it has lots of pictures of bears round the wall so I expect you'll feel at home." She led the way up a long flight of stairs, chattering all the time. Paddington followed closely behind, keeping carefully to the side so that he didn't have to tread on the carpet.

" That's the bathroom," said Judy. " And that's my room. And that's Jonathan's—he's my brother, and you'll meet him soon. And that's Mummy and Daddy's." She opened a door. " And this is going to be yours! "

Paddington nearly fell over with surprise when he

24

followed her into the room. He'd never seen such a big one. There was a large bed with white sheets against one wall and several big boxes, one with a mirror on it. Judy pulled open a drawer in one of the boxes. " This is called a chest of drawers," she said. " You'll be able to keep all your things in here."

Paddington looked at the drawer and then at his suitcase. " I don't seem to have very much. That's the trouble with being small—no one ever expects you to want things."

" Then we shall have to see what we can do," said Judy, mysteriously. " I'll try and get Mummy to take you on one of her shopping expeditions." She knelt down beside him. " Let me help you to unpack."

" It's very kind of you," Paddington fumbled with the lock. " But I don't think there's much to help me with. There's a jar of marmalade—only there's hardly any left now and what there is tastes of sea-weed. And my scrapbook. And some centavos— they're a sort of South American penny."

" Gosh! " said Judy. " I've never seen any of those before. Aren't they bright! "

" Oh, I keep them polished," said Paddington. " I don't *spend* them." He pulled out a tattered photograph. " And that's a picture of my Aunt Lucy. She had it taken just before she went into the home for retired bears in Lima."

" She looks very nice," said Judy. " And very wise." Seeing that Paddington had a sad, far-away

25

look in his eyes, she added hastily, " Well, I'm going to leave you now, so that you can have your bath and come down nice and clean. You'll find two taps, one marked hot and one marked cold. There's plenty of soap and a clean towel. Oh, and a brush so that you can scrub your back."

" It sounds very complicated," said Paddington. " Can't I just sit in a puddle or something? "

Judy laughed. " Somehow I don't think Mrs. Bird would approve of that! And don't forget to wash your ears. They look awfully black."

" They're meant to be black," Paddington called indignantly, as Judy shut the door.

He climbed up on to a stool by the window and looked out. There was a large, interesting garden below, with a small pond and several trees which looked good for climbing. Beyond the trees he could see some more houses stretching away into the distance. He decided it must be wonderful living in a house like this all the time. He stayed where he was, thinking about it, until the window became steamed up and he couldn't see out any more. Then he tried writing his name on the cloudy part with his paws. He began to wish it wasn't quite so long, as he soon ran out of cloud and it was rather difficult to spell.

" All the same "—he climbed on to the dressing-table and looked at himself in the mirror—" it's a very important name. I don't expect there are many bears in the world called Paddington! "

26

If he'd only known, Judy was saying exactly the same thing to Mr. Brown at that very moment. The Browns were holding a council of war in the dining-room, and Mr. Brown was fighting a losing battle. It had been Judy's idea in the first place to keep Paddington. In this she not only had Jonathan on her side but also her Mother. Jonathan had yet to meet Paddington but the idea of having a bear in the family appealed to him. It sounded very important.

"After all, Henry," argued Mrs. Brown, "you can't turn him out now. It wouldn't be right."

Mr. Brown sighed. He knew when he was beaten. It wasn't that he didn't like the idea of keeping Paddington. Secretly he was just as keen as anyone. But as head of the Brown household he felt he ought to consider the matter from every angle.

"I'm sure we ought to report the matter to someone first," he said.

"I don't see why, Dad," cried Jonathan. "Besides, he might get arrested for being a stowaway if we do that."

Mrs. Brown put down her knitting. "Jonathan's right, Henry. We can't let that happen. It's not as if he's done anything wrong. I'm sure he didn't harm anyone travelling in a lifeboat like that."

"Then there's the question of pocket money," said Mr. Brown, weakening. "I'm not sure how much pocket-money to give a bear."

" He can have one and sixpence a week, the same as the other children," replied Mrs. Brown.

Mr. Brown lit his pipe carefully before replying. " Well," he said, " we'll have to see what Mrs. Bird has to say about it first, of course."

There was a triumphant chorus from the rest of the family.

" You'd better ask her then," said Mrs. Brown, when the noise had died down. " It was your idea."

Mr. Brown coughed. He was a little bit afraid of Mrs. Bird and he wasn't at all sure how she would take it. He was about to suggest they left it for a little while when the door opened and Mrs. Bird herself came in with the tea things. She paused for a moment and looked round at the sea of expectant faces.

" I suppose," she said, " you want to tell me you've decided to keep that young Paddington."

" May we, Mrs. Bird? " pleaded Judy. " *Please!* I'm sure he'll be very good."

" Humph! " Mrs. Bird put the tray down on the table. " That remains to be seen. Different people have different ideas about being good. All the same," she hesitated at the door. " He looks the sort of bear that means well."

" Then you don't mind, Mrs. Bird? " Mr. Brown. asked her.

Mrs. Bird thought for a moment. " No. No, I don't mind at all. I've always had a soft spot for bears myself. It'll be nice to have one about the house."

28

" Well," gasped Mrs. Brown, as the door closed. " Whoever would have thought it! "

" I expect it was because he raised his hat," said Judy. " It made a good impression. Mrs. Bird likes polite people."

Mrs. Brown picked up her knitting again. " I suppose someone ought to write and tell his Aunt Lucy. I'm sure she'd like to know he's safe." She turned to Judy. " Perhaps it would be a nice thought if you and Jonathan wrote."

" By the way," said Mr. Brown, " come to think of it, where *is* Paddington? He's not still up in his room, is he? "

Judy looked up from the writing-desk, where she was searching for some notepaper. " Oh, he's all right. He's just having a bath."

" A *bath*! " Mrs. Brown's face took on a worried expression. " He's rather small to be having a bath all by himself."

" Don't fuss so, Mary," grumbled Mr. Brown, settling himself down in the armchair with a newspaper. " He's probably having the time of his life."

Mr. Brown was fairly near the truth when he said Paddington was probably having the time of his life. Unfortunately it wasn't in quite the way he meant it. Blissfully unaware that his fate was being decided, Paddington was sitting in the middle of the bathroom floor drawing a map of South America with a tube of Mr. Brown's shaving cream.

29

Paddington liked geography. At least, he liked *his* sort of geography, which meant seeing strange places and new people. Before he left South America on his long journey to England, his Aunt Lucy, who was a very wise old bear, had done her best to teach him all she knew. She had told him all about the places he would see on the way and she had spent many long hours reading to him about the people he would meet.

It had been a long journey, half-way round the world, and so Paddington's map occupied most of the bathroom floor and also used up most of Mr. Brown's shaving cream. With the little that was left he tried writing his new name again. He had several attempts and finally decided on PADINGTUN. It looked most important.

It wasn't until a trickle of warm water landed on his nose that he realised the bath was full and was beginning to run over the side. With a sigh he climbed up on to the side of the bath, closed his eyes, held his nose with one paw, and jumped. The water was hot and soapy and much deeper than he had expected. In fact, he had to stand on tiptoe even to keep his nose above the surface.

It was then that he had a nasty shock. It's one thing getting into a bath. It's quite another matter getting out, especially when the water comes up to your nose and the sides are slippery and your eyes are full of soap. He couldn't even see to turn the taps off.

He tried calling out " Help," first in quite a quiet

voice, then very loudly: " HELP! HELP! "

He waited for a few moments but no one came.
Suddenly he had an idea. What a good thing he was
still wearing his hat! He took it off and began baling
out the water.

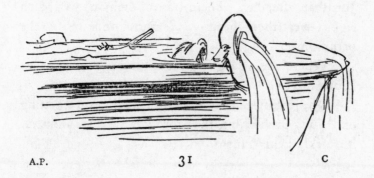

There were several holes in the hat because it was a very old one that had once belonged to his uncle, but if the water didn't get much less, at least it didn't get any more.

" That's funny," said Mr. Brown, jumping up from his armchair and rubbing his forehead. " I could have sworn I felt a spot of water! "

" Don't be silly, dear. How could you? " Mrs. Brown, busy with her knitting didn't even bother to look up.

Mr. Brown grunted and returned to his newspaper. He *knew* he had felt something, but there was no point in arguing. He looked suspiciously at the children, but both Judy and Jonathan were busy writing their letter.

" How much does it cost to send a letter to Lima? " asked Jonathan.

Judy was about to reply when another drop of water fell down from the ceiling, this time right on to the table.

" Oh, gosh! " she jumped to her feet, pulling Jonathan after her. There was an ominous wet patch right over their heads *and* right underneath the bathroom!

" Where are you going now, dear? " asked Mrs. Brown.

" Oh, just upstairs to see how Paddington's getting on." Judy pushed Jonathan through the door and shut it quickly behind them.

"Crikey," said Jonathan. "What's up?"

"It's Paddington," cried Judy over her shoulder as she rushed up the stairs. "I think he's in trouble!"

She ran along the landing and banged loudly on the bathroom door. "Are you all right, Paddington?" she shouted. "May we come in?"

"HELP! HELP!" shouted Paddington. "*Please* come in. I think I'm going to drown!"

"Oh, Paddington," Judy leant over the side of the bath and helped Jonathan lift a dripping and very frightened Paddington on to the floor. "Oh, Paddington! Thank goodness you're all right!"

Paddington lay on his back in a pool of water. "What a good job I had my hat," he panted. "Aunt Lucy told me never to be without it."

"But why on earth didn't you pull the plug out, you silly?" said Judy.

"Oh!" Paddington looked crestfallen. "I . . . I never thought of that."

Jonathan looked admiringly at Paddington. "Crikey," he said. "Fancy you making all this mess. Even *I've* never made as much mess as this!"

Paddington sat up and looked around. The whole of the bathroom floor was covered in a sort of white foam where the hot water had landed on his map of South America. "It *is* a bit untidy," he admitted. "I don't really know how it got like that."

"Untidy!" Judy lifted him to his feet and wrapped

33

a towel around him. "Paddington, we've all got a lot
of work to do before we go downstairs again. If Mrs.
Bird sees this I don't know what she'll say."

"I do," exclaimed Jonathan. "She says it to me
sometimes."

Judy began wiping the floor with a cloth. "Now

just you dry yourself quickly in case you catch cold."

Paddington began rubbing himself meekly with the
towel. "I must say," he remarked, looking at himself
in the mirror. "I *am* a lot cleaner than I was. It
doesn't look like me at all!"

Paddington *did* look much cleaner than when he
had first arrived at the Browns. His fur, which was
really quite light in colour and not dark brown as it
had been, was standing out like a new brush, except

34

that it was soft and silky. His nose gleamed and his ears had lost all traces of the jam and cream. He was so much cleaner that when he arrived downstairs and entered the dining-room some time later, everyone pretended not to recognise him.

"The tradesmen's entrance is at the side," said Mr. Brown, from behind his paper.

Mrs. Brown put down her knitting and stared at him. "I think you must have come to the wrong house," she said. "This is number thirty-two not thirty-four!"

Even Jonathan and Judy agreed there must be some mistake. Paddington began to get quite worried until they all burst out laughing and said how nice he looked now that he was brushed and combed and respectable.

They made room for him in a small armchair by the fire and Mrs. Bird came in with another pot of tea and a plate of hot, buttered toast.

"Now, Paddington," said Mr. Brown, when they were all settled. "Suppose you tell us all about yourself and how you came to Britain."

Paddington settled back in his armchair, wiped a smear of butter carefully from his whiskers, put his paws behind his head and stretched out his toes towards the fire. He liked an audience, especially when he was warm and the world seemed such a nice place.

"I was brought up in Darkest Peru," he began.

" By my Aunt Lucy. She's the one that lives in a home for retired bears in Lima." He closed his eyes thoughtfully.

A hush fell over the room and everyone waited expectantly. After a while, when nothing happened, they began to get restless. Mr. Brown coughed loudly. " It doesn't seem a very exciting story," he said, impatiently.

He reached across and poked Paddington with his pipe. " Well I never," he said. " I do believe he's fallen asleep! "

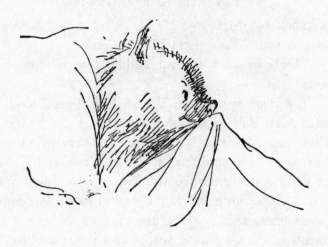

Paddington Goes Underground

PADDINGTON WAS very surprised when he woke up
the next morning and found himself in bed. He
decided it was a nice feeling as he stretched himself
and pulled the sheets up round his head with a paw.
He reached out with his feet and found a cool spot
for his toes. One advantage of being a very small
bear in a large bed was that there was so much
room.

After a few minutes he poked his head out cautiously
and sniffed. There was a lovely smell of something
coming under the door. It seemed to be getting
nearer and nearer. There were footsteps too, coming
up the stairs. As they stopped by his door there was

37

a knock and Mrs. Bird's voice called out, " Are you awake, young Paddington? "

" Only just," called out Paddington, rubbing his eyes.

The door opened. " You've had a good sleep," said Mrs. Bird as she placed a tray on the bed and drew the curtains. " And you're a very privileged person to have breakfast in bed on a *weekday*! "

Paddington eyed the tray hungrily. There was half a grapefruit in a bowl, a plate of bacon and eggs, some toast, and a whole pot of marmalade, not to mention a large cup of tea. " Is all that for me? " he exclaimed.

" If you don't want it I can soon take it away again," said Mrs. Bird.

" Oh, I do," said Paddington, hurriedly. " It's just that I've never seen so much breakfast before."

" Well, you'd better hurry up with it." Mrs. Bird turned in the doorway and looked back. " Because you're going on a shopping expedition this morning with Mrs. Brown and Judy. And all I can say is, thank goodness I'm not going too! " She closed the door.

" Now I wonder what she meant by that? " said Paddington. But he didn't worry about it for very long. There was far too much to do. It was the first time he had ever had breakfast in bed and he soon found it wasn't quite so easy as it looked. First of all he had trouble with the grapefruit. Every time he pressed it with his spoon a long stream of juice

shot up and hit him in the eye, which was very painful.
And all the time he was worried because the bacon
and eggs were getting cold. Then there was the
question of the marmalade. He wanted to leave
room for the marmalade.

In the end he decided it would be much easier if
he mixed everything up on the one plate and sat on
the tray to eat it.

"Oh, Paddington," said Judy when she entered
the room a few minutes later and found him perched
on the tray, "whatever are you doing now? Do
hurry up. We're waiting for you downstairs."

Paddington looked up, an expression of bliss on
his face; that part of his face which could be seen
behind eggy whiskers and toast crumbs. He tried

to say something but all he could manage was a muffled grunting noise which sounded like IMJUST-COMING all rolled into one.

" Really! " Judy took out her handkerchief and wiped his face. " You're the stickiest bear imagin-able. And if you don't hurry up all the nice things will be gone. Mummy's going to buy you a com-plete new outfit at Barkridges — I heard her say so. Now, comb your fur quickly and come on down."

As she closed the door Paddington looked at the remains of his breakfast. Most of it was gone but there was a large piece of bacon left which it seemed a pity to waste. He decided to put it into his suitcase in case he got hungry later on.

He hurried into the bathroom and rubbed his face over with some warm water. Then he combed his whiskers carefully and a few moments later, not looking perhaps as clean as he had done the evening before, but quite smart, he arrived downstairs.

" I hope you're not wearing that hat," said Mrs. Brown, as she looked down at him.

" Oh, do let him, Mummy," cried Judy. " It's so . . . so unusual."

" It's unusual all right," said Mrs. Brown. " I don't know that I've ever seen anything quite like it before. It's such a funny shape. I don't know what you'd call it."

" It's a bush hat," said Paddington, proudly. " And it saved my life."

" Saved your life? " repeated Mrs. Brown. " Don't be silly. How could a hat save your life? "

Paddington was about to tell her of his adventure in the bath the evening before when he received a nudge from Judy. She shook her head. " Er . . . it's a long story," he said, lamely.

" Then you'd better save it for another time," said Mrs. Brown. " Now, come along, both of you."

Paddington picked up his suitcase and followed Mrs. Brown and Judy to the front door. By the door Mrs. Brown paused and sniffed.

" That's very strange," she said. " There seems to be a smell of bacon everywhere this morning. Can *you* smell it, Paddington? "

Paddington started. He put the suitcase guiltily behind himself and sniffed. He had several expressions which he kept for emergencies. There was his thoughtful expression, when he stared into space and rested his chin on a paw. Then there was his innocent one which wasn't really an expression at all. He decided to use this one.

" It's very strong," he said, truthfully, for he was a truthful bear. And then he added, perhaps not quite so truthfully, " I wonder where it's coming from? "

" If I were you," whispered Judy, as they walked along the road towards the tube station, " I should be more careful in future when you pack your suitcase! "

Paddington looked down. A large piece of bacon

41

stuck out of the side of his case and was trailing on the pavement.

"Shoo!" cried Mrs. Brown as a grubby looking dog came bounding across the road. Paddington waved his suitcase. "Go away, dog," he said, sternly. The dog licked its lips and Paddington glanced anxiously over his shoulder as he hurried on, keeping close behind Mrs. Brown and Judy.

"Oh dear," said Mrs. Brown. "I have a funny feeling about to-day. As if *things* are going to happen. Do you ever have that feeling, Paddington?"

Paddington considered for a moment. "Sometimes," he said vaguely as they entered the station.

At first Paddington was a little bit disappointed in the Underground. He liked the noise and the bustle and the smell of warm air which greeted him as they went inside. But he didn't think much of the ticket.

He examined carefully the piece of green cardboard which he held in his paw. "It doesn't seem much to get for fourpence," he said. After all the lovely whirring and clanking noises the ticket machine had made it did seem disappointing. He'd expected much more for fourpence.

"But Paddington," Mrs. Brown sighed, "you only have a ticket so that you can ride on the train. They won't let you on otherwise." She looked and sounded rather flustered. Secretly she was beginning to wish they had waited until later in the day, when it wasn't quite so crowded. There was also the

peculiar business of the dogs. Not one, but six dogs of various shapes and sizes had followed them right inside. She had a funny feeling it had something to do with Paddington, but the only time she caught his eye it had such an innocent expression she felt quite upset with herself for having such thoughts.

" I suppose," she said to Paddington, as they stepped on the escalator, " we ought really to carry you. It says you're supposed to carry dogs but it doesn't say anything about bears."

Paddington didn't answer. He was following behind in a dream. Being a very short bear he couldn't easily see over the side, but when he did his eyes nearly popped out with excitement. There were people everywhere. He'd never seen so many. There were people rushing down one side and there were more people rushing up the other. Everyone seemed in a terrible hurry. As he stepped off the escalator he found himself carried away between a man with an umbrella and a lady with a large shopping bag. By the time he managed to push his way free both Mrs. Brown and Judy had completely disappeared.

It was then that he saw a most surprising notice. He blinked at it several times to make sure but each time he opened his eyes it said the same thing: FOLLOW THE AMBER LIGHT TO PADDINGTON.

Paddington decided the Underground was quite the most exciting thing that had ever happened to him. He turned and trotted down the corridor, following

43

the amber lights, until he met another crowd of people who were queueing for the ' up ' escalator.

" 'ere, 'ere," said the man at the top, as he examined Paddington's ticket. " What's all this? You haven't been anywhere yet! "

" I know," said Paddington, unhappily. " I think I must have made a mistake at the bottom."

The man sniffed suspiciously and called across to an inspector. " There's a young bear 'ere, smelling of bacon. Says he made a mistake at the bottom."

The inspector put his thumbs under his waistcoat. " Escalators is for the benefit and convenience of passengers," he said, sternly. " Not for the likes of young bears to play on. Especially in the rush hour."

" Yes, sir," said Paddington, raising his hat. " But we don't have esca . . . esca . . . "

" . . . lators," said the inspector, helpfully.

" . . . lators," said Paddington, " in Darkest Peru. I've never been on one before, so it's rather difficult."

" Darkest Peru? " said the inspector, looking most impressed. " Oh, well in that case "—he lifted up the chain which divided the ' up ' and the ' down ' escalators—" you'd better get back down. But don't let me catch you up to any tricks again."

" Thank you very much," said Paddington gratefully, as he ducked under the chain. " It's very kind of you, I'm sure." He turned to wave good-bye, but before he could raise his hat he found himself being whisked into the depths of the Underground again.

44

Half-way down he was gazing with interest at the brightly coloured posters on the wall when the man standing behind poked him with his umbrella. "There's someone calling you," he said.

Paddington looked round and was just in time to see Mrs. Brown and Judy pass by on their way up. They waved frantically at him and Mrs. Brown called out "Stop!" several times.

Paddington turned and tried to run up the escalator, but it was going very fast, and with his short legs it was as much as he could do even to stand still. He had his head down and he didn't notice a fat man with a briefcase who was running in the opposite direction until it was too late.

There was a roar of rage from the fat man and he toppled over and grabbed at several other people. Then Paddington felt himself falling. He went bump, bump, bump all the way down before he shot off the end and finally skidded to a stop by the wall.

When he looked round everything seemed very confused. A number of people were gathered round the fat man, who was sitting on the floor rubbing his head. Away in the distance he could see Mrs. Brown and Judy trying to push their way down the ' up ' escalator. It was while he was watching their efforts that he saw another notice. It was in a brass case at the bottom of the escalator and it said, in big red letters: TO STOP THE ESCALATOR IN CASES OF EMERGENCY PUSH THE BUTTON.

It also said in much smaller letters, ' Penalty for Improper Use—£5.' But in his hurry Paddington did not notice this. In any case it seemed to him very much of an emergency. He swung his suitcase through the air and hit the button as hard as he could.

If there had been confusion while the escalator was moving, there was even more when it stopped. Paddington watched with surprise as everyone started running about in different directions shouting at each other. One man even began calling out ' Fire!' and somewhere in the distance a bell began to ring.

He was just thinking what a lot of excitement pressing one small button could cause when a heavy hand descended on his shoulder.

"That's him!" someone shouted, pointing an accusing finger. "Saw him do it with me own eyes. As large as life!"

"Hit it with his suitcase," shouted another voice. "Ought not to be allowed!" While from the back of the crowd someone else suggested sending for the police.

Paddington began to feel frightened. He turned and looked up at the owner of the hand.

"Oh," said a stern voice. "It's *you* again. I might have known." The inspector took out a notebook. "Name, please."

"Er . . . Paddington," said Paddington.

"I said what's your name, not where do you want to go," repeated the inspector.

"That's right," said Paddington. "That *is* my name."

"*Paddington!*" said the inspector, disbelievingly. "It can't be. That's the name of a station. I've never heard of a bear called Paddington before."

"It's very unusual," said Paddington. "But it's Paddington Brown, and I live at number thirty-two Windsor Gardens. And I've lost Mrs. Brown and Judy."

"Oh!" The inspector wrote something in his book. "Can I see your ticket?"

"Er . . . I had it," said Paddington. "But I don't seem to any more."

The inspector began writing again. "Playing on

the escalator. Travelling without a ticket. *Stopping* the escalator. All serious offences they are." He looked up. "What have you got to say to that, young feller me lad?"

"Well . . . er . . ." Paddington shifted uneasily and looked down at his paws.

"Have you tried looking inside your hat?" asked the inspector, not unkindly. "People often put their tickets in there."

Paddington jumped with relief. "I knew I had it somewhere," he said, thankfully, as he handed it to the inspector.

The inspector handed it back again quickly. The inside of Paddington's hat was rather sticky.

"I've never known anyone take so long not to get anywhere," he said, looking hard at Paddington. "Do you often travel on the Underground?"

"It's the first time," said Paddington.

"And the last if I have anything to do with it," said Mrs. Brown as she pushed her way through the crowd.

"Is this your bear, Madam," asked the inspector. "Because if it is, I have to inform you that he's in serious trouble." He began to read from his notebook. "As far as I can see he's broken two important regulations—probably more. I shall have to give him into custody."

"Oh dear." Mrs. Brown clutched at Judy for support. "Do you *have* to? He's only small and

it's his first time out in London. I'm sure he won't do it again."

"Ignorance of the law is no excuse," said the inspector, ominously. "Not in court! Persons are expected to abide by the regulations. It says so."

"In court!" Mrs. Brown passed a hand nervously

over her forehead. The word court always upset her. She had visions of Paddington being taken away in handcuffs and being cross-examined and all sorts of awful things.

Judy took hold of Paddington's paw and squeezed it reassuringly. Paddington looked up gratefully. He wasn't at all sure what they were talking about, but none of it sounded very nice.

"Did you say *persons* are expected to abide by the regulations?" Judy asked, firmly.

49

" That's right," began the inspector. " And I have my duty to do the same as everyone else."

" But it doesn't say anything about bears? " asked Judy, innocently.

" Well," the inspector scratched his head. " Not in so many words." He looked down at Judy, then at Paddington, and then all around. The escalator had started up again and the crowd of sightseers had disappeared.

" It's all highly irregular," he said. " But . . ."

" Oh, thank you," said Judy. " I think you're the kindest man I've ever met! Don't *you* think so, Paddington? " Paddington nodded his head vigorously and the inspector blushed.

" I shall always travel on this Underground in future," said Paddington, politely. " I'm sure it's the nicest in all London."

The inspector opened his mouth and seemed about to say something, but he closed it again.

" Come along, children," said Mrs. Brown, hastily. " If we don't hurry up we shall never get our shopping done."

From somewhere up above came the sound of some dogs barking. The inspector sighed. " I can't understand it," he said. " This used to be such a well run, respectable station. Now look at it! "

He stared after the retreating figures of Mrs. Brown and Judy with Paddington bringing up the rear and then he rubbed his eyes. " That's funny," he said,

more to himself. " I must be seeing things. I could have sworn that bear had some bacon sticking out of his case! " He shrugged his shoulders. There were more important things to worry about. Judging by the noise coming from the top of the escalator there was some sort of dog fight going on. It needed investigating.

A Shopping Expedition

THE MAN in the gentlemen's outfitting department at Barkridges held Paddington's hat at arm's length between thumb and forefinger. He looked at it distastefully.

"I take it the young . . . er, gentleman, will not be requiring this any more, Modom?" he said.

"Oh yes, I shall," said Paddington, firmly. "I've always had that hat—ever since I was small."

"But wouldn't you like a nice new one, Pad-

dington?" said Mrs. Brown, adding hastily, "for *best*?"

Paddington thought for a moment. "I'll have one for *worst* if you like," he said. "*That*'s my best one!"

The salesman shuddered slightly and, averting his gaze, placed the offending article in the far end of the counter.

"Albert!" He beckoned to a youth who was hovering in the background. "See what we have in size $4\frac{7}{8}$." Albert began to rummage under the counter.

"And now, while we're about it," said Mrs. Brown, "we'd like a nice warm coat for the winter. Something like a duffle coat with toggles so that he can do it up easily, I thought. And we'd also like a plastic raincoat for the summer."

The salesman looked at her haughtily. He wasn't very fond of bears and this one, especially, had been giving him queer looks ever since he'd mentioned his wretched hat. "Has Modom tried the bargain basement?" he began. "Something in Government Surplus . . ."

"No, I haven't," said Mrs. Brown, hotly. "Government Surplus indeed! I've never heard of such a thing—have you, Paddington?"

"No," said Paddington, who had no idea what Government Surplus was. "*Never!*" He stared hard at the man, who looked away uneasily. Paddington had a very persistent stare when he cared

to use it. It was a very powerful stare. One which his Aunt Lucy had taught him and which he kept for special occasions.

Mrs. Brown pointed to a smart blue duffle coat with a red lining. " That looks the very thing," she said.

The assistant gulped. " Yes, Modom. Certainly, Modom." He beckoned to Paddington. " Come this way, sir."

Paddington followed the assistant, keeping about two feet behind him, and staring very hard. The back of the man's neck seemed to go a dull red and he fingered his collar nervously. As they passed the hat counter, Albert, who lived in constant fear of his superior, and who had been watching the events with an open mouth, gave Paddington the thumbs-up sign. Paddington waved a paw. He was beginning to enjoy himself.

He allowed the assistant to help him on with the coat and then stood admiring himself in the mirror. It was the first coat he had ever possessed. In Peru it had been very hot, and though his Aunt Lucy had made him wear a hat to prevent sunstroke, it had always been much too warm for a coat of any sort. He looked at himself in the mirror and was surprised to see not one, but a long line of bears stretching away as far as the eye could see. In fact, everywhere he looked there were bears, and they were all looking extremely smart.

" Isn't the hood a trifle large? " asked Mrs. Brown, anxiously.

" Hoods are being worn large this year, Modom," said the assistant. " It's the latest fashion." He was about to add that Paddington seemed to have rather a large head anyway but he changed his mind. Bears were rather unpredictable. You never quite knew what they were thinking and this one in particular seemed to have a mind of his own.

" Do *you* like it, Paddington? " asked Mrs. Brown. Paddington gave up counting bears in the mirror and turned round to look at the back view. " I think it's the nicest coat I've ever seen," he said, after a moment's thought. Mrs. Brown and the assistant heaved a sigh of relief.

" Good," said Mrs. Brown. " That's settled, then. Now there's just the question of a hat and a plastic mackintosh."

She walked over to the hat counter, where Albert, who could still hardly take his admiring eyes off Paddington, had arranged a huge pile of hats. There were bowler hats, sun hats, trilby hats, berets, and even a very small top hat. Mrs. Brown eyed them doubtfully. " It's difficult," she said, looking at Paddington. " It's largely a question of his ears. They stick out rather."

" You could cut some holes for them," said Albert.

The assistant froze him with a glance. " Cut a hole

in a *Barkridge*'s hat! " he exclaimed. " I've never heard of such a thing."

Paddington turned and stared at him. " I . . . er . . ." The assistant's voice trailed off. " I'll go and fetch my scissors," he said, in a queer voice.

" I don't think that will be necessary at all," said Mrs. Brown, hurriedly. " It's not as if he had to go to work in the city, so he doesn't want anything too smart. I think this woollen beret is very nice. The one with the pom-pom on top. The green will go well with his new coat and it'll stretch so that he can pull it down over his ears when it gets cold."

Everyone agreed that Paddington looked very smart, and while Mrs. Brown looked for a plastic mackintosh, he trotted off to have another look at himself in the mirror. He found the beret was a little difficult to raise as his ears kept the bottom half firmly in place. But by pulling on the pom-pom he could make it stretch quite a long way, which was almost as good. It meant, too, that he could be polite without getting his ears cold.

The assistant wanted to wrap up the duffle coat for him but after a lot of fuss it was agreed that, even though it was a warm day, he should wear it. Paddington felt very proud of himself and he was anxious to see if other people noticed.

After shaking hands with Albert, Paddington gave the assistant one more long, hard stare and the unfortunate man collapsed into a chair and began

mopping his brow as Mrs. Brown led the way out through the door.

Barkridges was a large shop and it even had its

own escalator as well as several lifts. Mrs. B hesitated at the door and then took Paddington's paw firmly in her hand and led him towards the lift. She'd had enough of escalators for one day.

But to Paddington everything was new, or almost everything, and he liked trying strange things. After a few seconds he decided quite definitely that he preferred riding on an escalator. They were nice and smooth. But lifts! To start with, it was full of people carrying parcels and all so busy they had no time to notice a small bear—one woman even rested her shopping bag on his head and seemed quite surprised

57

when Paddington pushed it off. Then, suddenly, half of him seemed to fall away while the other half stayed where it was. Just as he had got used to that feeling the second half of him caught up again and even overtook the first half before the doors opened. It did that four times on the way down and Paddington was glad when the man in charge said it was the ground floor and Mrs. Brown led him out.

She looked at him closely. " Oh dear, Paddington, you look quite pale," she said. " Are you all right? "

" I feel sick," said Paddington. " I don't like lifts. And I wish I hadn't had such a big breakfast! "

" Oh dear! " Mrs. Brown looked around. Judy, who had gone off to do some shopping of her own, was nowhere to be seen. " Will you be all right sitting here for a few minutes while I go off to find Judy? " she asked.

Paddington sank down on to his case looking very mournful. Even the pom-pom on his hat seemed limp.

" I don't know whether I shall be all right," he said. " But I'll do my best."

" I'll be as quick as I can," said Mrs. Brown. " Then we can take a taxi home for lunch."

Paddington groaned. "Poor Paddington," said Mrs. Brown, " you must be feeling bad if you don't want any lunch." At the word lunch again, Paddington

closed his eyes and gave an even louder groan. Mrs. Brown tiptoed away.

Paddington kept his eyes closed for several minutes and then, as he began to feel better, he gradually became aware that every now and then a nice cool draught of air blew over his face. He opened one eye carefully to see where it was coming from and noticed for the first time that he was sitting near the main entrance to the shop. He opened his other eye and decided to investigate. If he stayed just outside the glass door he could still see Mrs. Brown and Judy when they came.

And then, as he bent down to pick up his suitcase, everything suddenly went black. " Oh dear," thought Paddington, " now all the lights have gone out."

He began groping his way with outstretched paws towards the door. He gave a push where he thought it ought to be but nothing happened. He tried moving along the wall a little way and gave another push. This time it did move. The door seemed to have a strong spring on it and he had to push hard to make it open but eventually there was a gap big enough for him to squeeze through. It clanged shut behind him and Paddington was disappointed to find it was just as dark outside as it had been in the shop. He began to wish he'd stayed where he was. He turned round and tried to find the door but it seemed to have disappeared.

He decided it might be easier if he got down on his paws and crawled. He went a little way like this and then his head came up against something hard. He tried to push it to one side with his paw and it moved slightly so he pushed again.

Suddenly, there was a noise like thunder, and before he knew where he was a whole mountain of

things began to fall on him. It felt as if the whole sky had fallen in. Everything went quiet and he lay where he was for a few minutes with his eyes tightly shut, hardly daring to breathe. From a long way away he could hear voices and once or twice it sounded as if someone was banging on a window. He opened one eye carefully and was surprised to find the lights had come on again. At least . . . Sheepishly, he pushed the hood of his duffle coat up over his head.

They hadn't gone out at all! His hood must have fallen over his head when he bent down inside the shop to pick up his case.

Paddington sat up and looked around to see where he was. He felt much better now. Somewhat to his astonishment, he found he was sitting in a small room in the middle of which was a great pile of tins and basins and bowls. He rubbed his eyes and stared, round-eyed, at the sight.

Behind him there was a wall with a door in it, and in front of him there was a large window. On the other side of the window there was a large crowd of people pushing one another and pointing in his direction. Paddington decided with pleasure that they must be pointing at him. He stood up with difficulty, because it was hard standing up straight on top of a lot of tins, and pulled the pom-pom on his hat as high as it would go. A cheer went up from the crowd. Paddington gave a bow, waved several times, and then started to examine the damage all around him.

For a moment he wasn't quite sure where he was, and then it came to him. Instead of going out into the street he must have opened a door leading to one of the shop windows!

Paddington was an observant bear, and since he had arrived in London he'd noticed lots of these shop windows. They were very interesting. They always had so many things inside them to look at.

61

Once, he'd seen a man working in one, piling tin cans and boxes on top of each other to make a pyramid. He remembered deciding at the time what a nice job it must be.

He looked round thoughtfully. "Oh dear," he said to the world in general, "I'm in trouble again." If he'd knocked all these things down, as he supposed he must have done, someone was going to be cross. In fact, lots of people were going to be cross. People weren't very good at having things explained to them and it was going to be difficult explaining how his duffle coat hood had fallen over his head.

He bent down and began to pick up the things. There were some glass shelves lying on the floor where they had fallen. It was getting warm inside the window so he took off his duffle coat and hung it carefully on a nail. Then he picked up a glass shelf and tried balancing it on top of some tins. It seemed to work so he put some more tins and a washing-up bowl on top of that. It was rather wobbly but . . . he stood back and examined it . . . yes, it looked quite nice. There was an encouraging round of applause from outside. Paddington waved a paw at the crowd and picked up another shelf.

Inside the shop, Mrs. Brown was having an earnest conversation with the store detective.

"You say you left him here, Madam?" the detective was saying.

"That's right," said Mrs. Brown. "He was

feeling ill and I *told* him not to go away. His name's Paddington."

"Paddington." The detective wrote it carefully in his notebook. "What sort of bear is he?"

"Oh, he's sort of golden," said Mrs. Brown. "He was wearing a blue duffle coat and carrying a suit-case."

"And he has black ears," said Judy. "You can't mistake him."

"Black ears," the detective repeated, licking his pencil.

"I don't expect that'll help much," said Mrs. Brown. "He was wearing his beret."

The detective cupped his hand over his ear. "His *what?*" he shouted. There really was a terrible noise coming from somewhere. It seemed to be getting worse every minute. Every now and then there was a round of applause and several times he distinctly heard the sound of people cheering.

"His *beret*," shouted Mrs. Brown in return. "A green woollen one that came down over his ears. With a pom-pom."

The detective shut his notebook with a snap. The noise outside was definitely getting worse. "Pardon me," he said, sternly. "There's something queer going on that needs investigating."

Mrs. Brown and Judy exchanged glances. The same thought was running through both their minds. They both said "Paddington!" and rushed after the

detective. Mrs. Brown clung to the detective's coat and Judy clung to Mrs. Brown's as they forced their way through the crowd on the pavement. Just as they reached the window a tremendous cheer went up.

" I might have known," said Mrs. Brown.

" Paddington! " exclaimed Judy.

Paddington had just reached the top of his pyramid. At least, it had started off to be a pyramid, but it wasn't really. It wasn't any particular shape at all and it was very rickety. Having placed the last tin on the top Paddington was in trouble. He wanted to get down but he couldn't. He reached out a paw and the mountain began to wobble. Paddington clung helplessly to the tins, swaying to and fro, watched by a fascinated audience. And then, without any warning, the whole lot collapsed again, only this time Paddington was on top and not underneath. A groan of disappointment went up from the crowd.

" Best thing I've seen in years," said a man in the crowd to Mrs. Brown. " Blest if I know how they think these things up."

" Will he do it again, Mummy? " asked a small boy.

" I don't think so, dear," said his mother. " I think he's finished for the day." She pointed to the window where the detective was removing a sorry looking Paddington. Mrs. Brown hurried back to the entrance followed by Judy.

Inside the shop the detective looked at Paddington

and then at his notebook. "Blue duffle coat," he said. "Green woollen beret!" He pulled the beret off. "Black ears! I know who you are," he said grimly; "you're Paddington!"

Paddington nearly fell over backwards with astonishment.

"However did you know that?" he said.

"I'm a detective," said the man. "It's my job to know these things. We're always on the look-out for criminals."

"But I'm not a criminal," said Paddington, hotly. "I'm a bear! Besides, I was only tidying up the window . . ."

"Tidying up the window," the detective spluttered. "I don't know what Mr. Perkins will have to say. He only dressed it this morning."

Paddington looked round uneasily. He could see Mrs. Brown and Judy hurrying towards him. In fact, there were several people coming his way, including an important looking man in a black coat and striped trousers. They all reached him at the same time and all began talking together.

Paddington sat down on his case and watched them. There were times when it was much better to keep quiet, and this was one of them. In the end it was the important looking man who won, because he had the loudest voice and kept on talking when everyone else had finished.

To Paddington's surprise he reached down, took

hold of his paw, and started to shake it **so** hard he thought it was going to drop off.

"Delighted to know you, bear," he boomed "Delighted to know you. And congratulations."

"That's all right," said Paddington, doubtfully. He didn't know why, but the man seemed very pleased.

The man turned to Mrs. Brown. "You say his name's Paddington?"

"That's right," said Mrs. Brown. "And I'm sure he didn't mean any harm."

"Harm?" The man looked at Mrs. Brown in amazement. "Did you say *harm*? My dear lady, through the action of this bear we've had the biggest crowd in years. Our telephone hasn't stopped ringing." He waved towards the entrance to the store. "And still they come!"

He placed his hand on Paddington's head. "Barkridges," he said, "Barkridges is grateful!" He waved his other hand for silence. "We should like to show our gratitude. If there is anything . . . anything in the store you would like . . .?"

Paddington's eyes gleamed. He knew just what he wanted. He'd seen it on their way up to the outfitting department. It had been standing all by itself on a counter in the food store. The biggest one he'd ever seen. Almost as big as himself.

"Please," he said, "I'd like one of those jars of marmalade. One of the big ones."

66

If the manager of Barkridges felt surprised he didn't show it. He stood respectfully to one side, by the entrance to the lift.

"Marmalade it shall be," he said, pressing the button.

"I think," said Paddington, "if you don't mind, I'd rather use the stairs."

CHAPTER FIVE

Paddington and the ' Old Master '

PADDINGTON SOON settled down and became one of
the family. In fact, in no time at all it was difficult
to imagine what life had been like without him. He
made himself useful about the house and the days
passed quickly. The Browns lived near the Portobello
Road where there was a big market and quite often,
when Mrs. Brown was busy, she let him go out to
do the shopping for her. Mr. Brown made a shopping
trolley for him—an old basket on wheels with a
handle for steering it.

Paddington was a good shopper and soon became

68

well known to all the traders in the market. He was very thorough and took the job of shopping seriously. He would press the fruit to see that it had the right degree of firmness, as Mrs. Bird had shown him, and he was always on the look-out for bargains. He was a popular bear with the traders and most of them went out of their way to save the best things of the day for him.

" That bear gets more for his shilling than anyone I know," said Mrs. Bird. " I don't know how he gets away with it, really I don't. It must be the mean streak in him."

" I'm not mean," said Paddington, indignantly. " I'm just careful, that's all."

" Whatever it is," replied Mrs. Bird, " you're worth your weight in gold."

Paddington took this remark very seriously, and spent a long time weighing himself on the bathroom scales. Eventually he decided to consult his friend, Mr. Gruber, on the subject.

Now Paddington spent a lot of his time looking in shop windows, and of all the windows in the Portobello Road, Mr. Gruber's was the best. For one thing it was nice and low so that he could look in without having to stand on tiptoe, and for another, it was full of interesting things. Old pieces of furniture, medals, pots and pans, pictures; there were so many things it was difficult to get inside the shop, and old Mr. Gruber spent a lot of his time sitting in a deck-

chair on the pavement. Mr. Gruber, in his turn, found Paddington very interesting and soon they had become great friends. Paddington often stopped there on his way home from a shopping expedition and they spent many hours discussing South America, where Mr. Gruber had been when he was a boy. Mr. Gruber usually had a bun and a cup of cocoa in the morning for what he called his 'elevenses,' and he had taken to sharing it with Paddington. "There's nothing like a nice chat over a bun and a cup of cocoa," he used to say, and Paddington, who liked all three, agreed with him—even though the cocoa did make his whiskers go a funny colour.

Paddington was always interested in bright things and he had consulted Mr. Gruber one morning on the subject of his Peruvian centavos. He had an idea in the back of his mind that if they were worth a lot of money he could perhaps sell them and buy a present for the Browns. The one and sixpence a week pocket-money Mr. Brown gave him was nice, but by the time he had bought some buns on a Saturday morning there wasn't much left. After a great deal of consideration, Mr. Gruber had advised Paddington to keep the coins. "It's not always the brightest things that fetch the most money, Mr. Brown," he had said. Mr. Gruber always called Paddington 'Mr. Brown,' and it made him feel very important.

He had taken Paddington into the back of the shop where his desk was, and from a drawer he had

taken a cardboard box full of old coins. They had been rather dirty and disappointing. " See these, Mr. Brown? " he had said. " These are what they call sovereigns. You wouldn't think they were very valuable to look at them, but they are. They're made of gold and they're worth seventy shillings each. That's more than ten pounds for an ounce. If you ever find any of those, just you bring them to me."

One day, having weighed himself carefully on the scales, Paddington hurried round to Mr. Gruber, taking with him a piece of paper from his scrapbook, covered with mysterious calculations. After a big meal on a Sunday, Paddington had discovered he weighed nearly sixteen pounds. That was . . . he looked at his piece of paper again as he neared Mr. Gruber's shop . . . that was nearly two hundred and sixty ounces, which meant he was worth nearly two thousand five hundred pounds!

Mr. Gruber listened carefully to all that Paddington had to tell him and then closed his eyes and thought for a moment. He was a kindly man, and he didn't want to disappoint Paddington.

" I've no doubt," he said, at last, " that you're *worth* that. You're obviously a very valuable young bear. I know it. Mr. and Mrs. Brown know it. Mrs. Bird knows it. But do other people? "

He looked at Paddington over his glasses. " Things aren't always what they seem in this world, Mr. Brown," he said, sadly.

71

Paddington sighed. It was very disappointing. " I
wish they were," he said. " It would be so nice."

" Perhaps," said Mr. Gruber, mysteriously. " Perhaps. But we shouldn't have any nice surprises then,
should we? "

He took Paddington into his shop and after offering

him a seat disappeared for a moment. When he
returned he was carrying a large picture of a boat.
At least, half of it was a boat. The other half seemed
to be the picture of a lady in a large hat.

" There you are," he said, proudly. " That's what
I mean by things not always being what they seem.
I'd like your opinion on it, Mr. Brown."

Paddington felt rather flattered but also puzzled.

The picture didn't seem to be one thing or the other and he said so.

"Ah," said Mr. Gruber, delightedly. "It isn't at the moment. But just you wait until I've cleaned it! I gave five shillings for that picture years and years ago, when it was just a picture of a sailing ship. And what do you think? When I started to clean it the other day all the paint began to come off and I discovered there was another painting underneath." He looked around and then lowered his voice. "Nobody else knows," he whispered, "but I think the one underneath may be valuable. It may be what they call an 'old master.'"

Seeing that Paddington still looked puzzled, he explained to him that in the old days, when artists ran short of money and couldn't afford any canvas to paint on, they sometimes painted on top of old pictures. And sometimes, very occasionally, they painted them on top of pictures by artists who afterwards became famous and whose pictures were worth a lot of money. But as they had been painted over, no one knew anything about them.

"It all sounds very complicated," said Paddington thoughtfully.

Mr. Gruber talked for a long time about painting, which was one of his favourite subjects. But Paddington, though he was usually interested in anything Mr. Gruber had to tell him, was hardly listening. Eventually, refusing Mr. Gruber's offer of a second

cup of cocoa, he slipped down off the chair and began making his way home. He raised his hat automatically whenever anyone said good-day to him, but there was a far away expression in his eyes. Even the smell of buns from the bakery passed by unheeded. Paddington had an idea.

When he got home he went upstairs to his room and lay on the bed for a long while staring up at the ceiling. He was up there so long that Mrs. Bird became quite worried and poked her head round the door to know if he was all right.

"Quite all right, thank you," said Paddington, distantly. "I'm just thinking."

Mrs. Bird closed the door and hurried downstairs to tell the others. Her news had a mixed reception. "I don't mind him *just* thinking," said Mrs. Brown, with a worried expression on her face. "It's when he actually thinks *of* something that the trouble starts."

But she was in the middle of her housework and soon forgot the matter. Certainly both she and Mrs. Bird were much too busy to notice the small figure of a bear creeping cautiously in the direction of Mr. Brown's shed a few minutes later. Nor did they see him return armed with a bottle of Mr. Brown's paint remover and a large pile of rags. Had they done so they might have had good cause to worry. And if Mrs. Brown had seen him creeping on tiptoe into the drawing-room, closing the door carefully behind him, she wouldn't have had a minute's peace.

Fortunately everyone was much too busy to notice
any of these things. Even more fortunately, no one
came into the drawing-room for quite a long while.
Because Paddington was in a mess. Things hadn't
gone at all according to plan. He was beginning
to wish he had listened more carefully to the things
Mr. Gruber had said on the subject of cleaning
paintings.

To start with, even though he'd used almost half
a bottle of Mr. Brown's paint remover, the picture
had only come off in patches. Secondly, and what was
even worse, where it *had* come off there was nothing
underneath. Only the white canvas. Paddington
stood back and surveyed his handiwork. Originally
it had been a painting of a lake, with a blue sky and
several sailing boats dotted around. Now it looked

like a storm at sea. All the boats had gone, the sky was a funny shade of grey, and half the lake had disappeared.

"What a good thing I found this old box of paints," he thought, as he stood back holding the end of the brush at paw's length and squinting at it as he'd once seen a real artist do. Holding a palette in his left paw, he squeezed some red paint on to it and then splodged it about with the brush. He looked nervously over his shoulder and then dabbed some of it on to the canvas.

Paddington had found the paints in a cupboard under the stairs. A whole box of them. There were reds and greens and yellows and blues. In fact, there were

so many different colours it was difficult to know which to choose first.

He wiped the brush carefully on his hat and tried another colour and then another. It was all so interesting that he thought he would try a bit of each, and he very soon forgot the fact that he was supposed to be painting a picture.

In fact, it was more of a design than a picture, with lines and circles and crosses all in different colours. Even Paddington was startled when he finally stepped back to examine it. Of the original picture there was no trace at all. Rather sadly he put the tubes of paint back into the box and wrapped the picture in a canvas bag, leaning it against the wall, exactly as he'd found it. He decided reluctantly to have another try later on. Painting was fun while it lasted but it was much more difficult than it looked.

He was very silent all through dinner that evening. He was so silent that several times Mrs. Brown asked him how he was, until eventually Paddington asked to be excused and went upstairs.

" I do hope he's all right, Henry," she said, after he'd gone. " He hardly touched his dinner and that's so unlike him. And he seemed to have some funny red spots all over his face."

" Crikey," said Jonathan. " Red spots! I hope he's given it to me, whatever it is, then I shan't have to go back to school! "

"Well, he's got green ones as well," said Judy. "I saw some green ones!"

"*Green* ones!" Even Mr. Brown looked worried. "I wonder if he's sickening for anything? If they're not gone in the morning I'll send for the doctor."

"He was so looking forward to going to the handicrafts exhibition, too," said Mrs. Brown. "It'll be a shame if he has to stay in bed."

"Do you think you'll win a prize with your painting, Dad?" asked Jonathan.

"No one will be more surprised than your father if he does," replied Mrs. Brown. "He's never won a prize yet!"

"What is it, Daddy?" asked Judy. "Aren't you going to tell us?"

"It's meant to be a surprise," said Mr. Brown modestly. "It took me a long time to do. It's painted from memory."

Painting was one of Mr. Brown's hobbies, and once a year he entered a picture for a handicrafts exhibition which was held in Kensington, near where they lived. Several famous people came to judge the pictures and there were a number of prizes. There were also lots of other competitions, and it was a sore point with Mr. Brown that he had never won anything, whereas twice Mrs. Brown had won a prize in the rug-making competition.

"Anyway," he said, declaring the subject closed,

" it's too late now. The man collected it this afternoon, so we shall see what we shall see."

The sun was shining the next day and the exhibition
was crowded. Everyone was pleased that Paddington
looked so much better. His spots had completely
disappeared and he ate a large breakfast to make up
for missing so much dinner the night before. Only
Mrs. Bird had her suspicions when she found Paddington's ' spots ' on his towel in the bathroom, but
she kept her thoughts to herself.

The Browns occupied the middle five seats of the
front row where the judging was to take place. There
was an air of great excitement. It was news to
Paddington that Mr. Brown actually painted and he
was looking forward to seeing a picture by someone
he knew.

On the platform several important looking men
with beards were bustling about talking to each other
and waving their arms in the air. They appeared to
be having a great deal of argument about one painting
in particular.

" Henry," whispered Mrs. Brown, excitedly. " I
do believe they're talking about yours. I recognise
the canvas bag."

Mr. Brown looked puzzled. " It certainly looks
like my bag," he said. " But I don't think it can be.
All the canvas was stuck to the painting. Didn't you
see? Just as if someone had put it inside while it
was still wet. I painted mine ages ago."

Paddington sat very still and stared straight ahead, hardly daring to move. He had a strange sinking feeling in the bottom of his stomach, as if something awful was about to happen. He began to wish he hadn't washed his spots off that morning; then at least he could have stayed in bed.

Judy poked him with her elbow. " What's the matter, Paddington? " she asked. " You look most peculiar. Are you all right? "

" I don't feel ill," said Paddington in a small voice. " But I think I'm in trouble again."

" Oh dear," said Judy. " Well, keep your paws crossed. This is it! "

Paddington sat up. One of the men on the platform, the most important looking one with the biggest beard, was speaking. And there . . . Paddington's knees began to tremble . . . there, on the platform, on an easel in full view of everyone, was ' his ' picture!

He was so dazed he only caught scraps of what the man was saying.

" . . . remarkable use of colour . . ."

" . . . very unusual . . ."

" . . . great imagination . . . a credit to the artist . . ."

And then, he almost fell off his seat with surprise. " The winner of the first prize is Mr. Henry Brown of thirty-two Windsor Gardens! "

Paddington wasn't the only one who felt surprised. Mr. Brown, who was being helped up on to the

platform, looked as if he had just been struck by lightning. "But . . . but . . ." he stuttered, "there must be some mistake."

"Mistake?" said the man with the beard. "Nonsense, my dear sir. Your name's on the back of the canvas. You *are* Mr. Brown, aren't you? Mr. *Henry* Brown?"

Mr. Brown looked at the painting with unbelieving eyes. "It's certainly my name on the back," he said. "It's my writing . . ." He left the sentence unfinished and looked down towards the audience. He had his own ideas on the subject, but it was difficult to catch Paddington's eye. It usually was when you particularly wanted to.

"I think," said Mr. Brown, when the applause had died down, and he had accepted the cheque for ten pounds which the man gave him, "proud as I am,

I think I would like to donate the prize to a certain home for retired bears in South America." A murmur of surprise went round the assembly but it passed over Paddington's head, though he would have been very pleased had he known its cause. He was staring hard at the painting, and in particular at the man with the large beard, who was beginning to look hot and bothered.

"I think," said Paddington, to the world in general, "they might have stood it the right way up. It's not every day a bear wins first prize in a painting competition!"

CHAPTER SIX

A Visit to the Theatre

THE BROWNS were all very excited. Mr. Brown had
been given tickets for a box at the theatre. It was the
first night of a brand new play, and the leading part
was being played by the world famous actor, Sir Sealy
Bloom. Even Paddington became infected with the
excitement. He made several journeys to his friend,
Mr. Gruber, to have the theatre explained to him.
Mr. Gruber thought he was very lucky to be going
to the first night of a new play. " All sorts of famous
people will be there," he said. " I don't suppose
many bears have that sort of opportunity once in a
lifetime."

Mr. Gruber lent Paddington several second-hand

books about the theatre. He was rather a slow reader but there were lots of pictures, and in one of them, a big cut-out model of a stage which sprang up every time he opened the pages. Paddington decided that when he grew up he wanted to be an actor. He took to standing on his dressing-table and striking poses in the mirror just as he had seen them in the books.

Mrs. Brown had her own thoughts on the subject. " I *do* hope it's a nice play," she said to Mrs. Bird. " You know what Paddington's like . . . he does take these things so seriously."

" Oh, well," said Mrs. Bird, " *I* shall sit at home and listen to the wireless in peace and quiet. But it'll be an experience for him and he does like experiences so. Besides, he's been very good lately."

" I know," said Mrs. Brown. " That's what worries me! "

As it turned out, the play itself was the least of Mrs. Brown's worries. Paddington was unusually silent all the way to the theatre. It was the first time he had been out after dark and the very first time he had seen the lights of London. Mr. Brown pointed out all the famous landmarks as they drove past in the car, and it was a gay party of Browns that eventually trooped into the theatre.

Paddington was pleased to find it all exactly as Mr. Gruber had described it to him, even down to the commissionaire who opened the door for them and saluted as they entered the foyer.

Paddington returned the salute with a wave of his paw and then sniffed. Everything was painted red and gold and the theatre had a nice, warm, friendly sort of smell. There was a slight upset at the cloakroom when he found he had to pay sixpence in order to leave his duffle coat and suitcase. The woman behind the counter turned quite nasty when Paddington asked for his things back.

She was still talking about it in a loud voice as the attendant led them along a passage towards their seats. At the entrance to the box the attendant paused.

" Programme, sir? " she said to Paddington.

" Yes, please," said Paddington, taking five. " Thank you very much."

" And would you like coffee in the interval, sir? " she asked.

Paddington's eyes glistened. " Oh yes, please," he said, imagining it was a kind thought on the part of the theatre. He tried to push his way past, but the attendant barred the way.

" That'll be twelve and sixpence," she said. " Sixpence each for the programmes and two shillings each for the coffee."

Paddington looked as if he could hardly believe his ears. " Twelve shillings and sixpence? " he repeated. " *Twelve shillings and sixpence?* "

" That's all right, Paddington," said Mr. Brown, anxious to avoid another fuss. " It's my treat. You go in and sit down."

Paddington obeyed like a shot, but he gave the attendant some very queer looks while she arranged some cushions for his seat in the front row. All the same, he was pleased to see she had given him the one nearest the stage. He'd already sent a postcard to his Aunt Lucy with a carefully drawn copy of a plan of the theatre, which he'd found in one of Mr. Gruber's books, and a small cross in one corner marked 'MY SEET.'

The theatre was quite full and Paddington waved to the people down below. Much to Mrs. Brown's embarrassment, several of them pointed and waved back.

" I *do* wish he wouldn't be quite so friendly," she whispered to Mr. Brown.

" Wouldn't you like to take off your duffle coat now? " asked Mr. Brown. " It'll be cold when you go out again."

Paddington climbed up and stood on his chair. " I think perhaps I will," he said. " It's getting warm."

Judy started to help him off with it. " Mind my marmalade sandwich! " cried Paddington, as she placed it on the ledge in front of him. But it was too late. He looked round guiltily.

" Crikey! " said Jonathan. " It's fallen on some-one's head! " He looked over the edge of the box. " It's that man with the bald head. He looks jolly cross."

86

" Oh, Paddington! " Mrs. Brown looked despair-
ingly at him. " Do you *have* to bring marmalade
sandwiches to the theatre? "

" It's all right," said Paddington, cheerfully. " I've
some more in the other pocket if anyone wants one.
They're a bit squashed, I'm afraid, because I sat on
them in the car."

" There seems to be some sort of a row going on
down below," said Mr. Brown, craning his head to
look over the edge. " Some chap just waved his fist
at me. And what's all this about marmalade sandwiches? " Mr. Brown was a bit slow on the uptake
sometimes.

" Nothing, dear," said Mrs. Brown, hastily. She

decided to let the matter drop. In was much easier
in the long run.

In any case, Paddington was having a great struggle
with himself over some opera glasses. He had just
seen a little box in front of him marked OPERA GLASSES.
SIXPENCE. Eventually, after a great deal of thought,
he unlocked his suitcase and from a secret compartment withdrew a sixpence.

" I don't think much of these," he said, a moment
later, looking through them at the audience. " Everyone looks smaller."

" You've got them the wrong way round, silly,"
said Jonathan.

" Well, I still don't think much of them," said
Paddington, turning them round. " I wouldn't have
bought them if I'd known. Still," he added, after a
moment's thought. " They might come in useful
next time."

Just as he began to speak the overture came to
an end and the curtain rose. The scene was the
living room of a large house, and Sir Sealy Bloom,
in the part of a village squire, was pacing up and
down. There was a round of applause from the
audience.

" You don't take them home," whispered Judy.
" You have to put them back when you leave."

" WHAT! " cried Paddington, in a loud voice.
Several calls of ' hush ' came from the darkened
theatre as Sir Sealy Bloom paused and looked pointedly

in the direction of the Browns' box. " Do you mean to say . . ." words failed Paddington for the moment. " *Sixpence!* " he said, bitterly. " That's three buns' worth! " He turned his gaze on Sir Sealy Bloom.

Sir Sealy Bloom looked rather irritable. He didn't like first nights, and this one in particular had started badly. He had a nasty feeling about it. He much preferred playing the hero, where he had the sympathy of the audience, and in this play he was the villain. Being the first night of the play, he wasn't at all sure of some of his lines. To make matters worse, he had arrived at the theatre only to discover that the prompt boy was missing and there was no one else to take his place. Then there was the disturbance in the stalls just before the curtain went up. Something to do with a marmalade sandwich, so the stage manager had said. Of course, that was all nonsense, but still, it was very disturbing. And then there was this noisy crowd in the box. He sighed to himself. It was obviously going to be one of those nights.

But if Sir Sealy Bloom's heart was not in the play, Paddington's certainly was. He soon forgot about his wasted sixpence and devoted all his attention to the plot. He decided quite early on that he didn't like Sir Sealy Bloom and he stared at him hard through his opera glasses. He followed his every move and when, at the end of the first act, Sir Sealy, in the part of the hard-hearted father, turned his daughter out into the world without a penny, Pad-

dington stood up on his chair and waved his programme indignantly at the stage.

Paddington was a surprising bear in many ways
and he had a strong sense of right and wrong. As
the curtain came down he placed his opera glasses
firmly on the ledge and climbed off his seat.

" Are you enjoying it, Paddington? " asked Mr.
Brown.

" It's very interesting," said Paddington. He had
a determined note to his voice and Mrs. Brown looked
at him sharply. She was beginning to recognise that
tone and it worried her.

" Where are you going, dear? " she asked, as he
made for the door of the box.

" Oh, just out for a walk," said Paddington,
vaguely.

" Well, don't be too long," she called, as the door
closed behind him. " You don't want to miss any of
the second act."

" Oh, don't fuss, Mary," said Mr. Brown. " I
expect he just wants to stretch his legs or something.
He's probably gone out to the cloakroom."

But at that moment Paddington was going, not in
the direction of the cloakroom, but towards a door
leading to the back of the theatre. It was marked
PRIVATE. ARTISTS ONLY. As he pushed the door open
and passed through, he immediately found himself
in an entirely different world. There were no red
plush seats; everything was very bare. Lots of ropes

hung down from the roof, pieces of scenery were stacked against the walls, and everyone seemed in a great hurry. Normally Paddington would have been most interested in everything, but now he had a purposeful look on his face.

Seeing a man bending over some scenery, he walked over and tapped him on the shoulder. " Excuse me," he said. " Can you tell me where the man is? "

The scene hand went on working. " Man? " he said. " *What* man? "

" *The* man," said Paddington, patiently. " The nasty man."

" Oh, you mean Sir Sealy." The scene hand pointed towards a long corridor. " He's in his dressing-room. You'd better not go disturbing him 'cause he's not in a very good mood." He looked up. " Hey! " he cried. " You're not supposed to be in here. Who let you in? "

Paddington was too far away to answer even if he had heard. He was already half-way up the corridor, looking closely at all the doors. Eventually he came to one with a large star on it and the words SIR SEALY BLOOM in big gold letters. Paddington drew a deep breath and then knocked loudly. There was no reply, so he knocked again. Still there was no reply, and so, very cautiously, he pushed open the door with his paw.

" Go away! " said a booming voice. " I don't want to see anyone."

Paddington peered round the door. Sir Sealy Bloom was lying stretched out on a long couch. He looked tired and cross. He opened one eye and gazed at Paddington.

" I'm not signing any autographs," he growled.

" I don't want your autograph," said Paddington, fixing him with a hard stare. " I wouldn't want your autograph if I had my autograph book, and I haven't got my autograph book so there! "

Sir Sealy sat up. " You don't want my autograph? " he said, in a surprised voice. " But everyone always wants my autograph! "

" Well, I don't," said Paddington. " I've come to tell you to take your daughter back! " He gulped the last few words. The great man seemed to have grown to about twice the size he had been on the stage, and he looked as if he was going to explode at any minute.

Sir Sealy clutched his forehead. " You want me to take my daughter back? " he said at last.

" That's right," said Paddington, firmly. " And if you don't, I expect she can come and stay with Mr. and Mrs. Brown."

Sir Sealy Bloom ran his hand distractedly through his hair and then pinched himself. " Mr. and Mrs. *Brown*," he repeated in a dazed voice. He looked wildly round the room and then dashed to the door. " Sarah! " he called, in a loud voice. " Sarah, come in here at once! " He backed round the room until

he had placed the couch between himself and Paddington. "Keep away, bear!" he said, dramatically, and then peered at Paddington, for he was rather short-sighted. "You *are* a bear, aren't you?" he added.

"That's right," said Paddington. "From Darkest Peru!"

Sir Sealy looked at his woollen hat. "Well then," he said crossly, playing for time, "you ought to know better than to wear a green hat in my dressing-room. Don't you know green is a very unlucky colour in the theatre? Take it off at once."

"It's not my fault," said Paddington. "I wanted to wear my proper hat." He had just started to explain all about his hat when the door burst open and the lady called Sarah entered. Paddington immediately recognised her as Sir Sealy's daughter in the play.

"It's all right," he said. "I've come to rescue you."

"You've *what?*" The lady seemed most surprised.

"Sarah," Sir Sealy Bloom came out from behind the couch. "Sarah, protect me from this . . . this mad bear!"

"I'm not mad," said Paddington, indignantly.

"Then kindly explain what you are doing in my dressing-room," boomed the great actor.

Paddington sighed. Sometimes people were very slow to understand things. Patiently he explained it

all to them. When he had finished, the lady called Sarah threw back her head and laughed.

" I'm glad you think it's funny," said Sir Sealy.

" But darling, don't you see? " she said. " It's a great compliment. Paddington really believes you were throwing me out into the world without a penny. It shows what a great actor you are! "

Sir Sealy thought for a moment. " Humph! " he said, gruffly. " Quite an understandable mistake, I suppose. He looks a remarkably intelligent bear, come to think of it."

Paddington looked from one to the other. " Then you were only acting all the time," he faltered.

The lady bent down and took his paw. " Of course, darling. But it was very kind of you to come to my rescue. I shall always remember it."

" Well, I *would* have rescued you if you'd wanted it," said Paddington.

Sir Sealy coughed. " Are you interested in the theatre, bear? " he boomed.

" Oh, yes," said Paddington. " *Very* much. Except I don't like having to pay sixpence for everything. I want to be an actor when I grow up."

The lady called Sarah jumped up. " Why, Sealy darling," she said, looking at Paddington. " I've an idea! " She whispered in Sir Sealy's ear and then Sir Sealy looked at Paddington. " It's a bit unusual," he said, thoughtfully. " But it's worth a try. Yes, it's certainly worth a try! "

In the theatre itself the interval was almost at an end and the Browns were getting restless.

"Oh, dear," said Mrs. Brown. "I wonder where he's got to?"

"If he doesn't hurry up," said Mr. Brown, "he's going to miss the start of the second act."

Just then there was a knock at the door and an attendant handed a note to Mr. Brown. "A young bear gentleman asked me to give you this," he announced. "He said it was very urgent."

"Er . . . thank you," said Mr. Brown, taking the note and opening it.

"What does it say?" asked Mrs. Brown, anxiously. "Is he all right?"

Mr. Brown handed her the note to read. "Your guess is as good as mine," he said.

Mrs. Brown looked at it. It was hastily written in pencil and it said: I HAVE BEEN GIVEN A VERRY IMPORT-ANT JOB. PADINGTUN. P.S. I WILL TEL YOU ABOUT IT LAYTER.

"Now what on earth can that mean?" said Mrs. Brown. "Trust something unusual to happen to Paddington."

"I don't know," said Mr. Brown, settling back in his chair as the lights went down. "But I'm not going to let it spoil the play."

"I hope the second half is better than the first," said Jonathan. "I thought the first half was rotten. That man kept on forgetting his lines."

The second half *was* much better than the first. From the moment Sir Sealy strode on to the stage the theatre was electrified. A great change had come over him. He no longer fumbled over his lines, and people who had coughed all through the first half now sat up in their seats and hung on his every word.

When the curtain finally came down on the end of the play, with Sir Sealy's daughter returning to his arms, there was a great burst of applause. The curtain rose again and the whole company bowed to the audience. Then it rose while Sir Sealy and Sarah bowed, but still the cheering went on. Finally Sir Sealy stepped forward and raised his hand for quiet.

"Ladies and gentlemen," he said. "Thank you for your kind applause. We are indeed most grateful. But before you leave I would like to introduce the youngest and most important member of our company. A young . . . er, bear, who came to our rescue . . ." The rest of Sir Sealy's speech was drowned in a buzz of excitement as he stepped forward to the very front of the stage, where a small screen hid a hole in the boards which was the prompt box.

He took hold of one of Paddington's paws and pulled. Paddington's head appeared through the hole. In his other paw he was grasping a copy of the script.

"Come along, Paddington," said Sir Sealy. "Come and take your bow."

96

" I can't," gasped Paddington. " I think I'm stuck! "

And stuck he was. It took several stagehands, the fireman, and a lot of butter to remove him after the audience had gone. But he was far enough out to twist round and raise his hat to the cheering crowd before the curtain came down for the last time.

Several nights later, anyone going into Paddington's room would have found him sitting up in bed with his scrapbook, a pair of scissors, and a pot of paste. He was busy pasting in a picture of Sir Sealy Bloom, which the great man had signed: ' To Paddington, with grateful thanks.' There was also a signed picture from the lady called Sarah, and one of his proudest possessions—a newspaper cutting about the play headed PADDINGTON SAVES THE DAY!

Mr. Gruber had told him that the photographs were probably worth a bit of money, but after much thought he had decided not to part with them. In any case, Sir Sealy Bloom had given him his sixpence back *and* a pair of opera glasses.

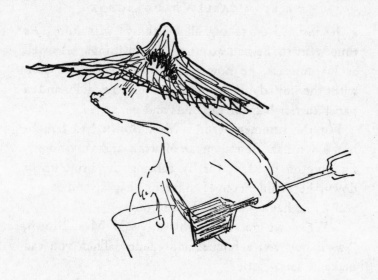

CHAPTER SEVEN

Adventure at the Seaside

ONE MORNING Mr. Brown tapped the barometer in the hall. " It looks as if it's going to be a nice day," he said. " How about a trip to the sea? "

His remark was greeted with enthusiasm by the rest of the family, and in no time at all the house was in an uproar.

Mrs. Bird started to cut a huge pile of sandwiches while Mr. Brown got the car ready. Jonathan and Judy searched for their bathing suits and Paddington went up to his room to pack. An outing which involved Paddington was always rather a business,

as he insisted on taking all his things with him. As time went by he had acquired lots of things. As well as his suitcase, he now had a smart week-end grip with the initials P.B. inscribed on the side and a paper carrier-bag for the odds and ends.

For the summer months Mrs. Brown had bought him a sun hat. It was made of straw and very floppy. Paddington liked it, for by turning the brim up or down, he could make it different shapes, and it was really like having several hats in one.

" When we get to Brightsea," said Mrs. Brown, " we'll buy you a bucket and spade. Then you can make a sand-castle."

" And you can go on the pier," said Jonathan, eagerly. " They've some super machines on the pier. You'd better bring plenty of pennies."

" And we can go swimming," added Judy. " You *can* swim, can't you? "

" Not very well, I'm afraid," replied Paddington. " You see, I've never been to the seaside before! "

" *Never* been to the seaside! " Everyone stopped what they were doing and stared at Paddington.

" Never," said Paddington.

They all agreed that it must be nice to be going to the seaside for the first time in one's life; even Mrs. Bird began talking about the time she first went to Brightsea, many years before. Paddington became very excited as they told him all about the wonderful things he was going to see.

The car was crowded when they started off. Mrs. Bird, Judy and Jonathan sat in the back. Mr. Brown drove and Mrs. Brown and Paddington sat beside him. Paddington liked sitting in the front, especially when the window was open, so that he could poke his head out in the cool breeze. After a minor delay when Paddington's hat blew off on the outskirts of London, they were soon on the open road.

" Can you smell the sea yet, Paddington? " asked Mrs. Brown after a while.

Paddington poked his head out and sniffed. " I can smell something," he said.

" Well," said Mr. Brown. " Keep on sniffing, because we're almost there." And sure enough, as they reached the top of a hill and rounded a corner to go down the other side, there it was in the distance, glistening in the morning sun.

Paddington's eyes opened wide. " Look at all the boats on the dirt! " he cried, pointing in the direction of the beach with his paw.

Everyone laughed. " That's not dirt," said Judy. " That's sand." By the time they had explained all about sand to Paddington they were in Brightsea itself, and driving along the front. Paddington looked at the sea rather doubtfully. The waves were much bigger than he had imagined. Not so big as the ones he'd seen on his journey to England, but quite large enough for a small bear.

Mr. Brown stopped the car by a shop on the

esplanade and took out some money. "I'd like to
fit this bear out for a day at the seaside," he said to
the lady behind the counter. "Let's see now, we
shall need a bucket and spade, a pair of sun-glasses,
one of those rubber tyres . . ." As he reeled off the
list, the lady handed the articles to Paddington, who
began to wish he had more than two paws. He had
a rubber tyre round his middle which kept slipping
down around his knees, a pair of sun-glasses balanced
precariously on his nose, his straw hat, a bucket and
spade in one hand, and his suitcase in the other.

"Photograph, sir?" Paddington turned to see an
untidy man with a camera looking at him. "Only a
shilling, sir. Results guaranteed. Money back if
you're not satisfied."

Paddington considered the matter for a moment.
He didn't like the look of the man very much, but
he had been saving hard for several weeks and now
had just over three shillings. It would be nice to
have a picture of himself.

"Won't take a minute, sir," said the man, disappearing behind a black cloth at the back of the
camera. "Just watch the birdie."

Paddington looked around. There was no bird in
sight as far as he could see. He went round behind
the man and tapped him. The photographer, who
appeared to be looking for something, jumped and
then emerged from under his cloth. "How do you
expect me to take your picture if you don't stand in

front?" he asked in an aggrieved voice. "Now I've wasted a plate, and "—he looked shiftily at Paddington —"that will cost you a shilling!"

Paddington gave him a hard stare. "You said there was a bird," he said. "And there wasn't."

"I expect it flew away when it saw your face," said the man nastily. "Now where's my shilling?"

Paddington looked at him even harder for a moment. "Perhaps the bird took it when it flew away," he said.

"Ha! Ha! Ha!" cried another photographer, who had been watching the proceedings with interest. "Fancy you being taken in by a bear, Charlie! Serves you right for trying to take photographs without a licence. Now be off with you before I call a policeman."

He watched while the other man gathered up his belongings and slouched off in the direction of the pier, then he turned to Paddington. "These people are a nuisance," he said. "Taking away the living from honest folk. You did quite right not to pay him any money. And if you'll allow me, I'd like to take a nice picture of you myself, as a reward!"

The Brown family exchanged glances. "I don't know," said Mrs. Brown. "Paddington always seems to fall on his feet."

"That's because he's a bear," said Mrs. Bird, darkly. "Bears always fall on their feet." She led the way on to the beach and carefully laid out a travelling rug on the sand behind a breakwater. "This will be as good a spot as any," she said.

103

" Then we shall all know where to come back to,
and no one will get lost."

" The tide's out," said Mr. Brown. " So it will be
nice and safe for bathing." He turned to Paddington.
" Are you going in, Paddington? " he asked.

Paddington looked at the sea. " I might go for a
paddle," he said.

" Well, hurry up," called Judy. " And bring your
bucket and spade, then we can practise making
sand-castles."

" Gosh! " Jonathan pointed to a notice pinned on
the wall behind them. " Look . . . there's a sand-castle
competition. Whizzo! First prize two pounds for
the biggest sand-castle! "

" Suppose we all join in and make one," said Judy.
" I bet the three of us together could make the biggest
one you've ever seen."

" I don't think you're allowed to," said Mrs.
Brown, reading the notice. " It says here everyone
has to make their own."

Judy looked disappointed. " Well, I shall have a
go, anyway. Come on, you two, let's have a bathe
first, then we can start digging after lunch." She
raced down the sand closely followed by Jonathan
and Paddington. At least, Jonathan followed but
Paddington only got a few yards before his lifebelt
slipped down and he went headlong in the sand.

" Paddington, *do* give me your suitcase," called
Mrs. Brown. " You can't take it in the sea with
you. It'll get wet and be ruined."

Looking rather crestfallen, Paddington handed his
things to Mrs. Brown for safekeeping and then ran
down the beach after the others. Judy and Jonathan
were already a long way out when he got there, so
he contented himself with sitting on the water's edge

for a while, letting the waves swirl around him as they came in. It was a nice feeling, a bit cold at first, but he soon got warm. He decided the seaside was a nice place to be. He paddled out to where the water was deeper and then lay back in his rubber tyre, letting the waves carry him gently back to the shore.

"Two pounds! Supposing . . . supposing he won two whole pounds!" He closed his eyes. In his mind he had a picture of a beautiful castle made of sand, like the one he'd once seen in a picture-book, with battlements and towers and a moat. It was getting bigger and bigger and everyone else on the beach had stopped to gather round and cheer. Several people said they had never seen such a big sand-castle, and . . . he woke with a start as he felt someone splashing water on him.

"Come on, Paddington," said Judy. "Lying there in the sun fast asleep. It's time for lunch, and we've got lots of work to do afterwards." Paddington felt disappointed. It had been a nice sand-castle in his

dream. He was sure it would have won first prize. He rubbed his eyes and followed Judy and Jonathan up the beach to where Mrs. Bird had laid out the sandwiches—ham, egg and cheese for every one else, and special marmalade ones for Paddington—with ice-cream and fruit salad to follow.

" I vote," said Mr. Brown, who had in mind an after-lunch nap for himself, " that after we've eaten, you all go off in different directions and make your own sand-castles. Then we'll have our own private competition as well as the official one. I'll give two shillings to the one with the biggest castle."

All three thought this was a good idea. " But don't go too far away," called Mrs. Brown, as Jonathan, Judy and Paddington set off. " Remember the tide's coming in! " Her advice fell on deaf ears; they were all much too interested in sand-castles. Paddington especially was gripping his bucket and spade in a very determined fashion.

The beach was crowded and he had to walk quite a long way before he found a deserted spot. First of all he dug a big moat in a circle, leaving himself a drawbridge so that he could fetch and carry the sand for the castle itself. Then he set to work carrying bucketloads of sand to build the walls of the castle.

He was an industrious bear and even though it was hard work and his legs and paws soon got tired, he persevered until he had a huge pile of sand in the middle of his circle. Then he set to work with his

spade, smoothing out the walls and making the battlements. They were very good battlements, with holes for windows and slots for the archers to fire through.

When he had finished he stuck his spade in one of the corner towers, placed his hat on top of that, and then lay down inside next to his marmalade jar and closed his eyes. He felt tired, but very pleased with himself. With the gentle roar of the sea in his ears he soon went fast asleep.

" We've been all along the beach," said Jonathan. " And we can't see him anywhere."

" He didn't even have his life-belt with him," said Mrs. Brown anxiously. " Nothing. Just a bucket and spade." The Browns were gathered in a worried group round the man from the lifesaving hut.

" He's been gone several hours," said Mr. Brown. " And the tide's been in over two! "

The man looked serious. " And you say he can't swim? " he asked.

" He doesn't even like having a bath much," said Judy. " So I'm sure he can't swim."

" Here's his photograph," said Mrs. Bird. " He only had it taken this morning." She handed the man Paddington's picture and then dabbed at her eyes with a handkerchief. " I know something's happened to him. He wouldn't have missed tea unless something was wrong."

The man looked at the picture. " We *could* send out a description," he said, dubiously. " But it's a job to see what he looks like by that. It's all hat and dark glasses."

" Can't you launch a lifeboat? " asked Jonathan, hopefully.

" We could," said the man. " If we knew where to look. But he might be anywhere."

" Oh, dear," Mrs. Brown reached for her handkerchief as well. " I can't bear to think about it."

" Something will turn up," said Mrs. Bird, comfortingly. " He's got a good head on his shoulders."

" Well," said the man, holding up a dripping straw hat. " You'd better have this, and in the meantime . . . we'll see what we can do."

" There, there, Mary! " Mr. Brown held his wife's arm. " Perhaps he just left it on the beach or something. It may have got picked up by the tide." He bent down to pick up the rest of Paddington's belongings. They seemed very small and lonely, lying there on their own.

" It's Paddington's hat all right," said Judy, examining it. " Look—it's got his mark inside! " She turned the hat inside out and showed them the outline of a paw mark in black ink and the words MY HAT—PADINGTUN.

" I vote we all separate," said Jonathan, " and comb the beach. We'll stand more chance that way."

Mr. Brown looked dubious. " It's getting dark," he said.

Mrs. Bird put down the travelling rug and folded her arms. " Well, I'm not going back until he's found," she said. " I couldn't go back to that empty house—not without Paddington."

" No one's thinking of going back without him, Mrs. Bird," said Mr. Brown. He looked helplessly out to sea. " It's just . . ."

" P'raps he didn't get swep' out to sea," said the lifesaving man, helpfully. " P'raps he's just gone on the pier or something. There seems to be a big crowd heading that way. Must be something interesting going on." He called out to a man who was just passing. " What's going on at the pier, chum? "

Without stopping the man looked back over his shoulder and shouted, " Chap just crossed the Atlantic all by 'isself on a raft. 'Undreds of days without food or water so they say! " He hurried on.

The lifesaving man looked disappointed. " Another of these publicity stunts," he said. " We get 'em every year."

Mr. Brown looked thoughtful. " I wonder," he said, looking in the direction of the pier.

" It would be just like him," said Mrs. Bird. " It's the sort of thing that would happen to Paddington."

" It's got to be! " cried Jonathan. " It's just got to be! "

They all looked at each other and then, picking up

their belongings, joined the crowd hurrying in the direction of the pier. It took them a long time to force their way through the turnstile, for the news that 'something was happening on the pier' had spread and there was a great throng at the entrance. But eventually, after Mr. Brown had spoken to a policeman, a way was made for them and they were escorted to the very end, where the paddle-steamers normally tied up.

A strange sight met their eyes. Paddington, who had just been pulled out of the water by a fisherman, was sitting on his upturned bucket talking to some reporters. Several of them were taking photographs while the rest fired questions at him.

"Have you come all the way from America?" asked one reporter.

The Browns, hardly knowing whether to laugh or cry, waited eagerly for Paddington's reply.

"Well, no," said Paddington, truthfully, after a moment's pause. "Not America. But I've come a long way." He waved a paw vaguely in the direction of the sea. "I got caught by the tide, you know."

"And you sat in that bucket all the time?" asked another man, taking a picture.

"That's right," replied Paddington. "And I used my spade as a paddle. It was lucky I had it with me."

"Did you live on plankton?" queried another voice.

Paddington looked puzzled. "No," he said. "Marmalade."

Mr. Brown pushed his way through the crowd. Paddington jumped up and looked rather guilty.

"Now then," said Mr. Brown, taking his paw. "That's enough questions for to-day. This bear's been at sea for a long time and he's tired. In fact," he looked meaningly at Paddington. "He's been at sea all the afternoon!"

"Is it still only Tuesday?" asked Paddington, innocently. "I thought it was much later than that!"

"Tuesday," said Mr. Brown, firmly. "And we've been worried to death over you!"

Paddington picked up his bucket and spade and jar of marmalade. "Well," he said. "I bet not many bears have gone to sea in a bucket, all the same."

It was dark when they drove along Brightsea front on their way home. The promenade was festooned with coloured lights and even the fountains in the gardens kept changing colour. It all looked very pretty. But Paddington, who was lying in the back of the car wrapped in a blanket, was thinking of his sand-castle.

"I bet mine was bigger than anyone else's," he said, sleepily.

"Bet you mine was the biggest," said Jonathan.

"I think," said Mr. Brown, hastily, "you'd all better have two shillings just to make sure."

"Perhaps we can come again another day," said

Mrs. Brown. "Then we can have another competition. How about that, Paddington?"

There was no reply from the back of the car. Sand-castles, paddling his bucket all across the harbour, and the sea air had proved too much for Paddington. He was fast asleep.

CHAPTER EIGHT

A Disappearing Trick

"Oooh," said Paddington, "is it really for me?"
He stared hungrily at the cake. It really was a
wonderful cake. One of Mrs. Bird's best. It was
covered with sugar icing and it had a cream and
marmalade filling. On the top there was one candle
and the words: TO PADDINGTON. WITH BEST WISHES
FOR A HAPPY BIRTHDAY—FROM EVERYONE.

It had been Mrs. Bird's idea to have a birthday
party. Paddington had been with them for two
months. No one, not even Paddington, knew quite

how old he was, so they decided to start again and call him one. Paddington thought this was a good idea, especially when he was told that bears had two birthdays every year—one in the summer and one in the winter.

" Just like the Queen," said Mrs. Bird. " So you ought to consider yourself very important."

Paddington did. In fact, he went round to Mr. Gruber straight away and told him the good news. Mr. Gruber looked impressed and was pleased when Paddington invited him to the party.

" It's not often anyone invites me out, Mr. Brown," he said. " I don't know when I went out last and I shall look forward to it very much indeed."

He didn't say any more at the time, but the next morning a van drew up outside the Browns' house and delivered a mysterious looking parcel from all the shopkeepers in the Portobello Market.

" Aren't you a lucky bear," exclaimed Mrs. Brown, when they opened the parcel and saw what was inside. It was a nice new shopping basket on wheels, with a bell on the side that Paddington could ring to let people know he was coming.

Paddington scratched his head. " It's a job to know what to do first," he said, as he carefully placed the basket with the other presents. " I shall have a lot of ' thank you ' letters to write."

" Perhaps you'd better leave them until to-morrow,"

said Mrs. Brown hastily. Whenever Paddington wrote any letters he generally managed to get more ink on himself than on the paper, and he was looking so unusually smart, having had a bath the night before, that it seemed a pity to spoil it.

Paddington looked disappointed. He liked writing letters. " Perhaps I can help Mrs. Bird in the kitchen," he said, hopefully.

" I'm glad to say," said Mrs. Bird, as she emerged from the kitchen, " that I've just finished. But you can lick the spoon if you like." She had bitter memories of other occasions when Paddington had ' helped ' in the kitchen. " But not too much," she warned, " or you won't have room for this."

It was then that Paddington saw his cake for the first time. His eyes, usually large and round, became so much larger and rounder, that even Mrs. Bird blushed with pride. " Special occasions demand special things," she said, and hurried off in the direction of the dining-room.

Paddington spent the rest of the day being hurried from one part of the house to another as preparations were made for his party. Mrs. Brown was busy tidying up. Mrs. Bird was busy in the kitchen. Jonathan and Judy were busy with the decorations. Everyone had a job except Paddington.

" I thought it was supposed to be *my* birthday," he grumbled, as he was sent packing into the drawing-

room for the fifth time after upsetting a box of marbles over the kitchen floor.

"So it is, dear," said a flustered Mrs. Brown. "But your time comes later." She was beginning to regret telling him that bears had two birthdays every year, for already he was worrying about when the next one was due.

"Now just you watch out of the window for the postman," she said, lifting him up on to the window sill. But Paddington didn't seem very keen on this. "Or else," she said, "practise doing some of your conjuring tricks, ready for this evening."

Among Paddington's many presents was a conjuring outfit from Mr. and Mrs. Brown. It was a very expensive one from Barkridges. It had a special magic table, a large mystery box which made things disappear if you followed the instructions properly, a magic wand and several packs of cards. Paddington emptied them all over the floor and settled down in the middle to read the book of instructions.

He sat there for a long time, studying the pictures and diagrams, and reading everything twice to make sure. Every now and then he absent-mindedly dipped a paw into his marmalade pot, and then, remembering it was his birthday and that there was a big tea to come, he reached up and stood the jar on the magic table before returning to his studies.

The first chapter was called SPELLS. It showed

how to wave the magic wand and the correct way to say ABRACADABRA. Paddington stood up, clutching the book in one paw, and waved the wand several times through the air. He also tried saying ABRACADABRA. He looked around. Nothing seemed to have changed, and he was just about to try again, when his eyes nearly popped out of his head. The jar of marmalade which he'd placed on the magic table only a few minutes before had disappeared!

He searched hurriedly through the book. There was nothing about making marmalade disappear. Worse still, there was nothing about making it come back again, either. Paddington decided it must be a very powerful spell to make a whole pot vanish into thin air.

He was about to rush outside and tell the others when he thought better of it. It might be a good trick to do in the evening, especially if he could persuade Mrs. Bird to give him another jar. He went out into the kitchen and waved his wand a few times in Mrs. Bird's direction, just to make sure.

" I'll give you ABRACADABRA," said Mrs. Bird, pushing him out again. " And be careful with that stick or you'll have someone's eye out."

Paddington returned to the drawing-room and tried saying his spell backwards. Nothing happened, so he started reading the next chapter of the instruction

book, which was called THE MYSTERY OF THE DIS-
APPEARING EGG.

" I shouldn't have thought you needed any book
to tell you that," said Mrs. Bird at lunch time, as
Paddington told them all about it. " The way you
gobble your food is nobody's business."

" Well," said Mr. Brown, " so long as you don't
try sawing anyone in half this evening, I don't
mind."

" I was only joking," he added hurriedly, as
Paddington turned an inquiring gaze on him. Nevertheless, as soon as lunch was over, Mr. Brown hurried
down the garden and locked up his tools. With
Paddington there was no sense in taking chances.

As it happened he had no cause to worry, for
Paddington had far too many things on his mind what
with one thing and another. The whole family were
there for tea as well as Mr. Gruber. Several other
people came along too, including the Browns' next
door neighbour, Mr. Curry. The last named was a
most unwelcome visitor. " Just because there's a free
tea," said Mrs. Bird. " I think it's disgusting, taking
the crumbs off a young bear's plate like that. He's
not even been invited! "

" He'll have to look slippy if he gets any crumbs
off Paddington's plate," said Mr. Brown. " All the
same, it *is* a bit thick, after all the things he's said in
the past. And not even bothering to wish him many
happy returns."

Mr. Curry had a reputation in the neighbourhood for meanness and for poking his nose into
other people's business. He was also very bad-
tempered, and was always complaining about the
least little thing which met with his disapproval.
In the past that had often included Paddington,
which was why the Browns had not invited him to
the party.

But even Mr. Curry had no cause to complain
about the tea. From the huge birthday cake down to
the last marmalade sandwich, everyone voted it was

the best tea they had ever had. Paddington himself
was so full he had great difficulty in mustering enough
breath to blow out the candle. But at last he managed
it without singeing his whiskers, and everyone,

including Mr. Curry, applauded and wished him a happy birthday.

"And now," said Mr. Brown, when the noise had died down. "If you'll all move your seats back, I think Paddington has a surprise for us."

While everyone was busy moving their seats to one side of the room, Paddington disappeared into the drawing-room and returned carrying his conjuring outfit. There was a short delay while he erected his magic table and adjusted the mystery box, but soon all was ready. The lights were turned off except for a standard lamp and Paddington waved his wand for quiet.

"Ladies and gentlemen," he began, consulting his instruction book, "my next trick is impossible!"

"But you haven't done one yet," grumbled Mr. Curry.

Ignoring the remark, Paddington turned over the page. "For this trick," he said. "I shall require an egg."

"Oh dear," said Mrs. Bird, as she hurried out to the kitchen, "I know something dreadful is going to happen."

Paddington placed the egg in the centre of his magic table and covered it with a handkerchief. He muttered ABRACADABRA several times and then hit the handkerchief with his wand.

Mr. and Mrs. Brown looked at each other. They were both thinking of their carpet. "Hey presto!"

said Paddington, and pulled the handkerchief away. To everyone's surprise the egg had completely disappeared.

" Of course," said Mr. Curry, knowledgeably, above the applause, " it's all done by sleight of paw. But very good though, for a bear. Very good indeed. Now make it come back again! "

Feeling very pleased with himself, Paddington took his bow and then felt in the secret compartment behind the table. To his surprise he found something much larger than an egg. In fact . . . it was a jar of marmalade. It was the one that had disappeared that very morning! He displayed it in his paw; the applause for this trick was even louder.

" Excellent," said Mr. Curry, slapping his knee. " Making people think he was going to find an egg, and it was a jar of marmalade all the time. Very good indeed! "

Paddington turned over a page. " And now," he announced, flushed with success, " the disappearing trick! " He took a bowl of Mrs. Brown's best flowers and placed them on the dining-table alongside his mystery box. He wasn't very happy about this trick, as he hadn't had time to practise it, and he wasn't at all sure how the mystery box worked or even where you put the flowers to make them disappear.

He opened the door in the back of the box and then poked his head round the side. " I shan't be a

minute," he said, and then disappeared from view again.

The audience sat in silence. " Rather a slow trick, this one," said Mr. Curry, after a while.

" I hope he's all right," said Mrs. Brown. " He seems very quiet."

" Well, he can't have gone far," said Mr. Curry. " Let's try knocking." He got up, knocked loudly on the box, and then put his ear to it. " I can hear someone calling," he said. " It sounds like Paddington. I'll try again." He shook the box and there was an answering thump from inside.

" I think he's shut himself in," said Mr. Gruber. He too knocked on the box and called out, "Are you all right, Mr. Brown ? "

" NO! " said a small and muffled voice. " It's all dark and I can't read my instruction book."

" Quite a good trick," said Mr. Curry, some while later, after they had prised open Paddington's mystery box with a penknife. He helped himself to some biscuits. " The disappearing bear. Very unusual! But I still don't see what the flowers were for."

Paddington looked at him suspiciously, but Mr. Curry was far too busy with the biscuits.

" For my next trick," said Paddington, " I would like a watch."

" Are you sure? " asked Mrs. Brown, anxiously. " Wouldn't anything else do? "

Paddington consulted his instruction book. "It says a watch," he said, firmly.

Mr. Brown hurriedly pulled his sleeve down over his left wrist. Unfortunately, Mr. Curry, who was in an unusually good mood after his free tea, stood up and offered his. Paddington took it gratefully and placed it on the table. "This is a jolly good trick," he said, reaching down into his box and pulling out a small hammer.

He covered the watch with a handkerchief and then hit it several times. Mr. Curry's expression froze. "I hope you know what you're doing, young bear," he said.

Paddington looked rather worried. Having turned over the page he'd just read the ominous words, "It is necessary to have a second watch for this trick." Gingerly, he lifted up a corner of the handkerchief. Several cogs and some pieces of glass rolled across the table. Mr. Curry let out a roar of wrath.

"I think I forgot to say ABRACADABRA," faltered Paddington.

"ABRACADABRA!" shouted Mr. Curry, beside himself with rage. "ABRACADABRA!" He held up the remains of his watch. "Twenty years I've had this watch, and now look at it! This will cost someone a pretty penny!"

Mr. Gruber took out an eyeglass and examined the watch carefully. "Nonsense," he said, coming to

Paddington's rescue. " It's one you bought from me for five shillings six months ago! You ought to be ashamed of yourself, telling lies in front of a young bear! "

" Rubbish! " spluttered Mr. Curry. He sat down heavily on Paddington's chair. " Rubbish! I'll give you . . ." his voice trailed away and a peculiar expression came over his face. " I'm sitting on something," he said. " Something wet and sticky! "

" Oh dear," said Paddington. " I expect it's my disappearing egg. It must have reappeared! "

Mr. Curry grew purple in the face. " I've never been so insulted in my life," he said. "Never! " He turned at the door and waved an accusing finger at the company. " It's the last time I shall ever come to one of *your* birthday parties! "

" Henry," said Mrs. Brown, as the door closed behind Mr. Curry, " you really oughtn't to laugh."

Mr. Brown tried hard to keep a straight face. " It's no good," he said, bursting out. " I can't help it."

" Did you see his face when all the cogs rolled out? " said Mr. Gruber, his face wet with tears.

" All the same," said Mr. Brown, when the laughter had died down. " I think perhaps you ought to try something a little less dangerous next time, Paddington."

" How about that card trick you were telling me about, Mr. Brown? " asked Mr. Gruber. " The one

where you tear up a card and make it come out of someone's ear."

"Yes, that sounds a nice quiet one," said Mrs. Brown. "Let's see that."

"You wouldn't like another disappearing trick?" asked Paddington, hopefully.

"Quite sure, dear," said Mrs. Brown.

"Well," said Paddington, rummaging in his box, "it's not very easy doing card tricks when you've only got paws, but I don't mind trying."

He offered a pack of cards to Mr. Gruber, who solemnly took one from the middle and then memorised it before replacing the card. Paddington waved his wand over the pack several times and then withdrew a card. He held up the seven of spades. "Was this it?" he said to Mr. Gruber.

Mr. Gruber polished his glasses and stared. "You know," he said, "I do believe it was!"

"I bet all the cards are the same," whispered Mr. Brown to his wife.

"Ssh!" said Mrs. Brown. "I thought he did it very well."

"This is the difficult bit," said Paddington, tearing it up. "I'm not very sure about this part." He put the pieces under his handkerchief and tapped them several times with the wand.

"Oh!" said Mr. Gruber, rubbing the side of his head. "I felt something go pop in my ear just then. Something cold and hard." He felt in his ear. "Why,

I do believe . . ." he held up a shining round object to the audience. " It's a sovereign! My birthday present for Paddington! Now I wonder how it got in there? "

" Oooh! " said Paddington, as he proudly examined it. " I didn't expect that. Thank you very much, Mr. Gruber."

" Well," said Mr. Gruber. " It's only a small present I'm afraid, Mr. Brown. But I've enjoyed the little chats we've had in the mornings. I look forward to them very much and, er," he cleared his throat and looked around, " I'm sure we all hope you have many more birthdays! "

When the chorus of agreement had died down, Mr. Brown rose and looked at the clock. " And now," he said, " it's long past all our bedtimes, most of all yours, Paddington, so I suggest we all do a disappearing trick now."

" I wish," said Paddington, as he stood at the door waving everyone good-bye, " I wish my Aunt Lucy could see me now. She'd feel very pleased."

" You'll have to write and tell her all about it, Paddington," said Mrs. Brown, as she took his paw. " But in the morning," she added hastily. " You've got clean sheets, remember."

" Yes," said Paddington. " In the morning. I expect if I did it now I'd get ink over the sheets or something. Things are always happening to me."

" You know, Henry," said Mrs. Brown, as they watched Paddington go up the stairs to bed, looking rather sticky and more than a little sleepy, " it's nice having a bear about the house."

More About Paddington

CONTENTS

CHAPTER ONE

A Family Group

THE BROWNS' HOUSE at number thirty-two Windsor Gardens was unusually quiet. It was a warm summer day and all the family with the exception of Paddington, who had mysteriously disappeared shortly after lunch, were sitting on the veranda enjoying the afternoon sun.

Apart from the faint rustle of paper as Mr. Brown turned the pages of an enormous book and the click of Mrs. Brown's knitting needles, the only sound came from Mrs. Bird, their housekeeper, as she prepared the tea things.

Jonathan and Judy were both much too busy piecing together a huge jig-saw puzzle to utter a word.

It was Mr. Brown who first broke the silence. "You know," he began, taking a long draw at his pipe, "it's a funny thing, but I've been through this encyclopædia a dozen times and there's no mention of a bear like Paddington."

"Ah, and there won't be," exclaimed Mrs. Bird. "Bears like Paddington are very rare. And a good thing too, if you ask me, or it would cost us a small fortune in marmalade." Mrs. Bird was always going on about Paddington's fondness for marmalade, but it was noticeable she was never without a spare jar in the larder in case of emergency.

"Anyway, Henry," said Mrs. Brown, as she put down her knitting, "why do you want to look up Paddington?"

Mr. Brown twirled his moustache thoughtfully. "Oh, no reason in particular," he answered, vaguely. "I was interested—that's all."

Having a bear in the family was a heavy responsibility—especially a bear like Paddington—and Mr. Brown took the matter very seriously.

"The point is," he said, snapping the book shut, "if he's staying with us for good . . ."

"*If*?" There was a chorus of alarm from the rest of the family, not to mention Mrs. Bird.

"What on earth do you mean, Henry?" exclaimed Mrs. Brown. "*If* Paddington is staying with us for good. Of course he is."

" *As* he's staying with us," said Mr. Brown, hastily, " there are one or two things I have in mind. First of all I've been thinking of decorating the spare room for him."

There was general agreement at this. Ever since he had first arrived on the scene Paddington had occupied the guest room. Being a polite bear he had never said anything, even when he'd been turned out to make room for visitors, but it had long been thought he should have a room of his own.

" The second thing," continued Mr. Brown, " is a photograph. I think it would be nice if we could have a family group taken."

" A photograph ? " exclaimed Mrs. Bird. " What a funny thing you should say that."

" Oh ? " said Mr. Brown. " Why's that ? "

Mrs. Bird busied herself with the teapot. " You'll see—all in good time," she said. And try as they might that was all the others could get from her.

Fortunately, she was saved any further questions, for at that moment there came a loud banging noise from the direction of the dining-room and Paddington himself appeared at the french windows. He was struggling with a large cardboard box, across the top of which lay a mysterious-looking metal object with long spikes on one end.

But it wasn't so much what he was carrying that caused a gasp of astonishment from the others. It was his general appearance.

His fur had an unusually soft, golden look about it, and his ears, or as much of them as they could see poking out from beneath the wide brim of his old hat, were as black and shiny as the tip of his nose. Even his paws and whiskers had to be seen to be believed.

Everyone sat up in amazement and Mrs. Brown dropped several stitches.

"Good heavens!" spluttered Mr. Brown, nearly spilling his tea over the encyclopædia. "What *have* you been doing to yourself?"

"I've been having a bath," said Paddington, looking most offended.

"A *bath*?" repeated Judy, slowly. "Without being asked?"

"Crikey!" said Jonathan. "We'd better put the flags out."

"You *are* all right?" asked Mr. Brown. "I mean—you're not feeling ill or anything?"

Paddington became even more injured at the excitement he had caused. It wasn't as if he *never* had a wash. In fact he had one most mornings. It was simply that he had decided views on baths in particular. Having a bath meant getting his fur wet all over and it took a long time to dry. "I only wanted to look nice for the photograph," he said, firmly.

"The photograph?" everyone echoed. It was really uncanny the way Paddington knew about things.

"Yes," said Paddington. An important expression came over his face as he bent down and started undoing

136

the string round his cardboard box. " I've bought myself a camera."

There was a moment's silence while the Browns watched the back view of Paddington bending over the box.

" A camera," said Mrs. Brown at last. " But aren't they very expensive?"

" This one wasn't," said Paddington, breathing hard. He stood up, clutching the biggest camera the Browns had ever seen. " I bought it at a sale in the market. It was only three and sixpence!"

" Three and sixpence!" exclaimed Mr. Brown, looking most impressed. He turned to the others. " I must say I've never known a bear with such an eye for a bargain as Paddington."

" Gosh!" said Jonathan. " It's got a hood to put over your head and everything."

" What's that long thing?" asked Judy.

" That's a tripod," explained Paddington, proudly. He sat down on the floor and began unfolding the legs. " It's to stand the camera on so that it doesn't shake."

Mr. Brown picked up the camera and examined it. As he turned it over some rusty screws and several old nails fell out. " Isn't it rather old?" he asked, without thinking. " It looks as if someone's been using it as a workbox instead of a camera."

Paddington lifted the brim of his hat and gave Mr. Brown a hard stare. " It's a very rare sort," he replied. " The man in the bargain shop said so."

"Well, *I* think it's super," exclaimed Jonathan, excitedly. "Bags you take my picture first, Paddington."

"I've only got one plate," said Paddington, decidedly. "Extra ones cost a lot and I haven't any pocket money left—so I'm afraid you'll all have to be in a group."

"It certainly looks most complicated, and rather

large for a bear," remarked Mrs. Brown, as Paddington screwed the camera on to the tripod and then adjusted the legs so that they were the right height. "Are you sure you'll be able to work it?"

"I think so," said Paddington. His voice became muffled as he disappeared underneath the black hood at the back. "Mr. Gruber lent me a book all about photography and I've been practising under the bedclothes."

Mr. Gruber, who kept an antique shop in the Portobello market, was a close friend of Paddington and
helped him with all his problems.

"Well, in that case"—Mr. Brown took charge of
the situation—"I suggest we all go on to the lawn and
let Paddington take our picture while the sun's shining."
And he led the way outside while Paddington bustled
around erecting his camera and tripod.

In a few moments Paddington announced that everything was ready and he began arranging the group as
he wanted them, running back to the camera every now
and then to peer at them through the lens.

Because the camera was so near the ground he had to
put Mr. Brown crouching in a rather uncomfortable
position behind Jonathan and Judy, with Mrs. Brown
and Mrs. Bird sitting on either side.

Although he didn't say anything, Paddington was a
bit disappointed with the view through the camera. He
could just recognise Mr. Brown because of his moustache,
but the others were much more difficult. Everyone
seemed blurred, almost as if they were standing in a
fog. It was strange, for when he took his head out of
the cloth it was quite sunny outside.

The Browns waited patiently while Paddington sat
on the grass and consulted his instruction book. Almost
at once he discovered a very interesting chapter headed
FOCUS. It explained how, if you wanted nice clear
pictures, it was important to make sure the camera was
the right distance away, and properly adjusted. It

even had a picture showing a man measuring the distance with a piece of string.

Several minutes went by, for Paddington was rather a slow reader, and there were a number of diagrams to examine.

" I hope he's not too long," said Mr. Brown. " I think I've got cramp coming on."

" He'll be disappointed if you move," said Mrs. Brown. " He took such a lot of trouble arranging us all and it really looks very nice."

" That's all very well," grumbled Mr. Brown. " You're sitting down."

" Ssh! " replied Mrs. Brown. " I think he's almost

ready now. He's doing something with a piece of string."

" What on earth is that for? " asked Mr. Brown.

" It's to measure you," said Paddington, tying a loop in the end.

" Well, if you don't mind," protested Mr. Brown, when he saw what Paddington was up to, " I'd much rather you tied the *other* end on to the camera instead of *this* end to my ear! " The rest of his sentence disappeared in a gurgle as Paddington pulled the string tight.

Paddington looked rather surprised and examined the knot round Mr. Brown's ear with interest. " I think I must have made a slip knot by mistake," he announced eventually. Paddington wasn't very good at knots—mainly because having paws made things difficult for him.

" Really, Henry," said Mrs. Brown. " Don't make such a fuss. Anyone would think you'd been hurt."

Mr. Brown rubbed his ear, which had gone a funny mauve colour. " It's *my* ear," he said, " and it jolly well does hurt."

" Now where's he going? " exclaimed Mrs. Bird, as Paddington hurried off towards the house.

" I expect he's gone to measure the string," said Jonathan.

" Huh! " said Mr. Brown. " Well, I'm going to stand up."

" Henry! " said Mrs. Brown. " If you do I shall be very cross."

"It's too late anyway," groaned Mr. Brown. "My leg's gone to sleep."

Luckily for Mr. Brown, Paddington arrived back at that moment. He stared hard at the sun and then at the waiting group. "I'm afraid you'll all have to come over here," he said, after consulting his instruction book. "The sun's moved."

"I'm not surprised," grumbled Mr. Brown, as he sat on the lawn rubbing his leg. "At the rate we're going it will have set before we're finished."

"I never realised having a picture taken could be so complicated," said Mrs. Bird.

"What I'm not sure about," whispered Judy, "is why Paddington bothered having a bath if *he's* taking the photograph."

"That's a point," said Mr. Brown. "How *are* you going to be in the picture, Paddington?"

Paddington gave Mr. Brown a strange look. That was something he hadn't thought of either, but he decided to meet that difficulty when it came. He had a lot of other important things to do first. "I'm going to press the shutter," he said, after a moment's thought, "and then run round the other side."

"But even bears can't run *that* fast," persisted Mr. Brown.

"I'm sure Paddington knows best, Henry," whispered Mrs. Brown. "And even if he doesn't, for goodness sake don't say anything. If he finds out he's had a bath for nothing we shall never hear the last of it."

142

" It seems a very long hood," said Mrs. Bird, looking towards the camera. " I can't see Paddington at all."

"That's because he's small," explained Jonathan. " He's had to lower the tripod."

The Browns sat very still with a fixed smile on their faces as Paddington came out from beneath his hood.

He made some complicated adjustments to the front of the camera and then, after announcing he was about to fit the photographic plate, disappeared again.

Suddenly, to everybody's surprise, the camera and tripod began to rock backwards and forwards in a most dangerous manner.

" Good gracious! " exclaimed Mrs. Bird. " Whatever's happening now? "

" Look out! " shouted Mr. Brown. " It's coming towards us."

They all stood up and moved away, staring with wide-open eyes at the camera as it followed them. But when it got to within several feet it suddenly stopped, then turned left and headed towards a rose bush.

" I do hope he's all right," said Mrs. Brown, anxiously.

" I wonder if we ought to do anything? " said Mrs. Bird, as there was a muffled cry from Paddington.

But before anyone could reply the camera rebounded from the rose bush and shot back across the lawn. It went twice round the pond in the middle and then jumped up in the air several times before toppling over, to land with a dull thud in the middle of Mr. Brown's best flower bed.

" Good heavens! " shouted Mr. Brown, as he rushed forward. " My petunias! "

"Never mind your petunias, Henry," exclaimed Mrs. Brown. "What about Paddington?"

"Well, no wonder," said Mr. Brown as he bent down and lifted the hood. "He's got his head stuck inside the camera!"

"I should be careful, Dad," said Jonathan as Mr. Brown began pulling at Paddington's legs. "His whiskers might be caught in the shutter."

Mr. Brown stopped pulling and crawled round to peer through the lens. "I can't see anything," he said after a moment's pause. "It's all dark inside." He tapped the case and there came another faint cry from within.

"Butter!" said Mrs. Bird, hurrying towards the kitchen. "There's nothing like butter when anyone's stuck." Mrs. Bird was a great believer in butter. She had used it several times in the past when Paddington had got himself stuck.

All the same, even with Jonathan holding one end and Mr. Brown pulling on the other, it was some while before Paddington's head finally came away from the camera. He sat on the grass rubbing his ears and looking very crestfallen. Things hadn't gone at all according to plan.

"I vote," said Mr. Brown, when order had finally been restored, "that we set everything up exactly as it was before and tie a string to the shutter. Then Paddington can sit in the group with us and work it from a distance. It'll be much safer that way."

Everyone agreed that this was a good idea, and while Mr. Brown arranged the group once again, Paddington busied himself setting up his camera and fitting the photographic plate inside it—making sure to stand well back this time. There was a slight setback when he pulled the string too hard and the tripod fell over, but finally the big moment arrived. There was a click from the camera and everyone relaxed.

The man in the photographic shop looked most surprised when Mrs. Bird, all the Browns and Paddington trooped in through the door a little later.

" It's certainly a very rare sort," he said, examining Paddington's camera with interest. " Very rare. I've read about them of course—but I've never actually seen one before. It . . . it must have been kept in a pantry or something. It seems to have a lot of butter inside it."

" I had a bit of an accident when I tried to put the plate in," said Paddington.

" We're all very anxious to see the result of the photograph," added Mr. Brown, hastily. " We were wondering if you could do it for us while we wait."

The man said he would be only too pleased to oblige. From all he had seen and heard he was quite eager to see the picture, and he hurried off to his dark room leaving the Browns alone in the shop. He couldn't remember ever having a young bear photographer in the shop before.

When he returned there was a puzzled expression on

his face. " You did say you took this picture to-day? " he asked, looking through the window at the bright sunshine.

" That's right," said Paddington, eyeing him suspiciously.

" Well, sir "—the man held the plate up to the light for Paddington to see—" it's nice and sharp—and I can certainly see you all—but it looks as if it was foggy at the time. And these patches of light—like moonbeams—they're very odd! "

Paddington took the plate from the man and examined it carefully. " I expect that's where I had my torch on under the bedclothes," he said at last.

" Well, I think it's a very nice picture for a first attempt," said Mrs. Bird. " And I'd like six postcard prints, please. I'm sure Paddington's Aunt Lucy in Peru would love one. She lives in the home for retired bears in Lima," she added, for the benefit of the shopkeeper.

" Does she? " said the man, looking most impressed. " Well, it's the first time I've ever had any pictures sent overseas—especially to a home for retired bears in Peru."

He thought for a moment. " I tell you what," he said, " if I could borrow this camera for a week to put in my shop window, I'll not only do all the prints you want but I'll take a photograph of each of you into the bargain. How's that? "

" I might have known," said Mr. Brown, as they were walking home, " that if Paddington took our

photographs something odd would happen. Fancy getting all these pictures for nothing! "

" Bears always fall on their feet," said Mrs. Bird, looking at Paddington.

But Paddington wasn't listening. He was still thinking about his camera.

Early next morning he hurried down to the shop and was pleased to see it already occupied a position of honour in the middle of the window.

Underneath it was a notice which said: A VERY RARE TYPE OF EARLY CAMERA—NOW OWNED BY MR. PADDINGTON BROWN—A YOUNG LOCAL BEAR GENTLEMAN.

But Paddington was even more pleased by another notice next to it which said: AN EXAMPLE OF HIS WORK— and underneath that was his picture.

It was a little blurred and there were several paw marks near the edge, but one or two people in the neighbourhood came up and congratulated him and several of them said they could quite clearly recognise everyone in it. All in all Paddington thought it had been a very good three-and-sixpence worth.

CHAPTER TWO

A Spot of Decorating

PADDINGTON GAVE a deep sigh and pulled his hat down over his ears in an effort to keep out the noise. There was such a hullabaloo going on it was difficult to write up the notes in his scrapbook.

The excitement had all started when Mr. and Mrs. Brown and Mrs. Bird received an unexpected invitation to a wedding. Luckily both Jonathan and Judy were out for the day or things might have been far worse. Paddington hadn't been included in the invitation, but he didn't really mind. He didn't like weddings very

much—apart from the free cake—and he'd been promised a piece of that whether he went or not.

All the same, he was beginning to wish everyone would hurry up and go. He had a special reason for wanting to be alone that day.

He sighed again, wiped the pen carefully on the back of his paw, and then mopped up some ink blots which somehow or other had found their way on to the table. He was only just in time, for at that moment the door burst open and Mrs. Brown rushed in.

" Ah, there you are, Paddington! " She stopped short in the middle of the room and stared at him. " Why on earth are you wearing your hat indoors? " she asked. " And why is your tongue all blue? "

Paddington stuck out his tongue as far as he could. " It *is* a funny colour," he admitted, squinting down at it with interest. " Perhaps I'm sickening for something! "

" You'll be sickening for something all right if you don't clear up this mess," grumbled Mrs. Bird as she entered. " Just look at it. Bottles of ink. Glue. Bits of paper. My best sewing scissors. Marmalade all over the table runner, and goodness knows what else."

Paddington looked around. It *was* in a bit of a state.

" I've almost finished," he announced. " I've just got to rule a few more lines and things. I've been writing my memories."

Paddington took his scrapbook very seriously and spent many long hours carefully pasting in pictures and writing up his adventures. Since he'd been at the Browns

so much had happened it was now more than half full.

"Well, make sure you *do* clear everything up," said Mrs. Brown, "or we shan't bring you back any cake. Now do take care of yourself. And don't forget—when the baker comes we want two loaves." With that she waved good-bye and followed Mrs. Bird out of the room.

"You know," said Mrs. Bird, as she stepped into the car, "I have a feeling that bear has something up his paw. He seemed most anxious for us to leave."

"Oh, I don't know," said Mrs. Brown. "I don't see what he *can* do. We shan't be away all that long."

"Ah!" replied Mrs. Bird, darkly. "That's as may be. But he's been hanging about on the landing upstairs half the morning. I'm sure he's up to something."

Mr. Brown, who didn't like weddings much either, and was secretly wishing he could stay at home with Paddington, looked over his shoulder as he let in the clutch. "Perhaps I ought to stay as well," he said. "Then I could get on with decorating his new room."

"Now, Henry," said Mrs. Brown, firmly. "You're coming to the wedding and that's that. Paddington will be quite all right by himself. He's a very capable bear. And as for your wanting to get on with decorating his new room . . . you haven't done a thing towards it for over a fortnight, so I'm sure it can wait another day."

Paddington's new room had become a sore point in the Brown household. It was over two weeks since Mr.

Brown had first thought of doing it. So far he had stripped all the old wallpaper from the walls, removed the picture rails, the wood round the doors, the door handle, and everything else that was loose, or that he had made loose, and bought a lot of bright new wallpaper, some whitewash and some paint. There matters had rested.

In the back of the car Mrs. Bird pretended she hadn't heard a thing. An idea had suddenly come into her mind and she was hoping it hadn't entered Paddington's as well; but Mrs. Bird knew the workings of Paddington's mind better than most and she feared the worst. Had she but known, her fears were being realised at that very moment. Paddington was busy scratching out the words " AT A LEWSE END " in his scrapbook and was adding, in large capital letters, the ominous ones: " DECKERATING MY NEW ROOM! "

It was while he'd been writing " AT A LEWSE END " in

his scrapbook earlier in the day that the idea had come to him. Paddington had noticed in the past that he often got his best ideas when he was " at a loose end."

For a long while all his belongings had been packed away ready for the big move to his new room, and he was beginning to get impatient. Every time he wanted anything special he had to undo yards of string and brown paper.

Having underlined the words in red, Paddington cleared everything up, locked his scrapbook carefully in his suitcase, and hurried upstairs. He had several times offered to lend a paw with the decorating, but for some reason or other Mr. Brown had put his foot down on the idea and hadn't even allowed him in the room while work was in progress. Paddington couldn't quite understand why. He was sure he would be very good at it.

The room in question was an old box-room which had been out of use for a number of years, and when he entered it, Paddington found it was even more interesting than he had expected.

He closed the door carefully behind him and sniffed. There was an exciting smell of paint and whitewash in the air. Not only that, but there were some steps, a trestle table, several brushes, a number of rolls of wallpaper, and a big pail of whitewash.

The room had a lovely echo as well, and he spent a long time sitting in the middle of the floor while he was stirring the paint, just listening to his new voice.

There were so many different and interesting things around that it was a job to know what to do first. Eventually Paddington decided on the painting. Choosing one of Mr. Brown's best brushes, he dipped it into the pot of paint and then looked round the room for something to dab it on.

It wasn't until he had been working on the window-frame for several minutes that he began to wish he had started on something else. The brush made his arm ache, and when he tried dipping his paw in the paint pot instead and rubbing it on, more paint seemed to go on to the glass than the wooden part, so that the room became quite dark.

"Perhaps," said Paddington, waving the brush in the air and addressing the room in general, "perhaps if I do the ceiling first with the whitewash I can cover all the drips on the wall with the wallpaper."

But when Paddington started work on the whitewashing he found it was almost as hard as painting. Even by standing on tip-toe at the very top of the steps, he had a job to reach the ceiling. The bucket of whitewash was much too heavy for him to lift, so that he had to come down the steps every time in order to dip the brush in. And when he carried the brush up again, the whitewash ran down his paw and made his fur all matted.

Looking around him, Paddington began to wish he was still "at a loose end." Things were beginning to

get in rather a mess again. He felt sure Mrs. Bird would have something to say when she saw it.

It was then that he had a brainwave. Paddington was a resourceful bear and he didn't like being beaten by things. Recently he had become interested in a house which was being built nearby. He had first seen it from the window of his bedroom and since then he'd spent many hours talking to the men and watching while they hoisted their tools and cement up to the top floor by means of a rope and pulley. Once, Mr. Briggs, the foreman, had even taken him up in the bucket too, and had let him lay several bricks.

Now the Browns' house was an old one and in the middle of the ceiling there was a large hook where a big lamp had once hung. Not only that, but in one corner of the room there was a thin coil of rope as well. . . .

Paddington set to work quickly. First he tied one end of the rope to the handle of the bucket. Then he climbed up the steps and passed the other end through the hook in the ceiling. But even so, when he had climbed down again, it still took him a long time to pull the bucket anywhere near the top of the steps. It was full to the brim with whitewash and very heavy, so that he had to stop every few seconds and tie the other end of the rope to the steps for safety.

It was when he undid the rope for the last time that things started to go wrong. As Paddington closed his eyes and leaned back for the final pull he suddenly felt to his surprise as if he was floating on air. It was a most

strange feeling. He reached out one foot and waved it around. There was definitely nothing there. He opened one eye and then nearly let go of the rope in astonishment as he saw the bucket of whitewash going past him on its way down.

Suddenly everything seemed to happen at once. Before he could even reach out a paw or shout for help, his head hit the ceiling and there was a clang as the bucket hit the floor.

For a few seconds Paddington clung there, kicking the air and not knowing what to do. Then there was a gurgling sound from below. Looking down, he saw to

his horror that all the whitewash was running out of the bucket. He felt the rope begin to move again as the bucket got lighter, and then it shot past him again as he descended to land with a bump in the middle of a sea of whitewash.

Even then his troubles weren't over. As he tried to regain his balance on the slippery floor, he let go of the rope, and with a rushing noise the bucket shot downwards again and landed on top of his head, completely covering him.

Paddington lay on his back in the whitewash for several minutes, trying to get his breath back and wondering what had hit him. When he did sit up and take the bucket off his head he quickly put it back on again. There was whitewash all over the floor, the paint pots had been upset into little rivers of brown and green, and Mr. Brown's decorating cap was floating in one corner of the room. When Paddington saw it he felt very glad he'd left *his* hat downstairs.

One thing was certain—he was going to have a lot of explaining to do. And that was going to be even more difficult than usual, because he couldn't even explain to himself quite what had gone wrong.

It was some while later, when he was sitting on the upturned bucket thinking about things, that the idea of doing the wallpapering came to him. Paddington had a hopeful nature and he believed in looking on the bright side. If he did the wallpapering really well, the others might not even notice the mess he'd made.

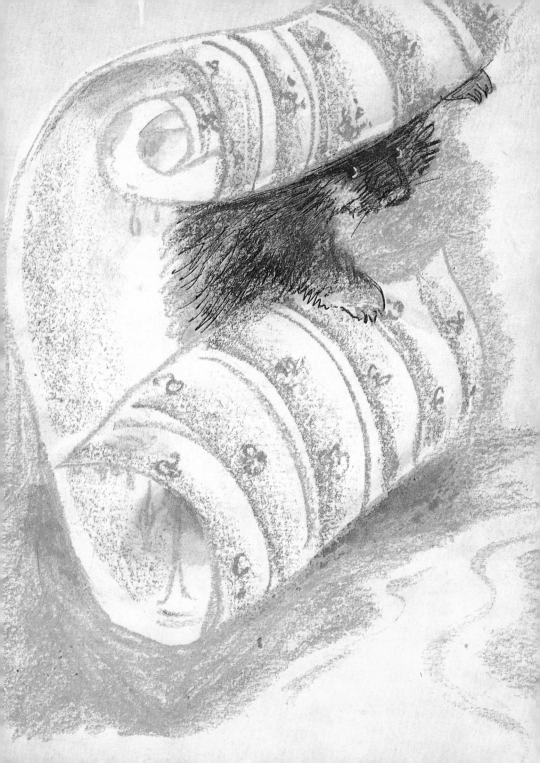

Paddington was fairly confident about the wall-papering. Unknown to Mr. Brown, he had often watched him in the past through a crack in the door, and it looked quite simple. All you had to do was to brush some sticky stuff on the back of the paper and then put it on the wall. The high parts weren't too difficult, even for a bear, because you could fold the paper in two and put a broom in the middle where the fold was. Then you simply pushed the broom up and down the wall in case there were any nasty wrinkles.

Paddington felt much more cheerful now he'd thought of the wallpapering. He found some paste already mixed in another bucket, which he put on top of the trestle while he unrolled the paper. It was a little diffi-cult at first because every time he tried to unroll the paper he had to crawl along the trestle pushing it with his paws and the other end rolled up again and followed behind him. But eventually he managed to get one piece completely covered in paste.

He climbed down off the trestle, carefully avoiding the worst of the whitewash, which by now was beginning to dry in large lumps, and lifted the sheet of wallpaper on to a broom. It was a long sheet of paper, much longer than it had seemed when he was putting the paste on, and somehow or other, as Paddington waved the broom about over his head, it began to wrap itself around him. After a struggle he managed to push his way out and headed in the general direction of a piece of wall. He stood back and surveyed the result. The

paper was torn in several places, and there seemed to be a lot of paste on the outside, but Paddington felt quite pleased with himself. He decided to try another piece, then another, running backwards and forwards between the trestle and the walls as fast as his legs could carry

him in an effort to get it all finished before the Browns returned.

Some of the pieces didn't quite join, others overlapped, and on most of them there were some very odd-looking patches of paste and whitewash. None of the pieces were as straight as he would have liked, but when he put his head on one side and squinted, Paddington felt

the overall effect was quite nice, and he felt very pleased
with himself.

It was as he was taking a final look round the room
at his handiwork that he noticed something very strange.
There was a window, and there was also a fireplace. But
there was no longer any sign of a door. Paddington
stopped squinting and his eyes grew rounder and rounder.
He distinctly remembered there *had* been a door because
he had come through it. He blinked at all four walls.
It was difficult to see properly because the paint on the
window-glass had started to dry and there was hardly
any light coming through—but there most definitely
wasn't a door!

" I can't understand it," said Mr. Brown as he entered
the dining-room. " I've looked everywhere and there's
no sign of Paddington. I told you I should have stayed
at home with him."

Mrs. Brown looked worried. " Oh dear, I hope
nothing's happened to him. It's so unlike him to go
out without leaving a note."

" He's not in his room," said Judy.

" Mr. Gruber hasn't seen him either," added Jonathan. " I've just been down to the market and he says
he hasn't seen him since they had cocoa together this
morning."

" Have *you* seen Paddington anywhere? " asked Mrs.
Brown as Mrs. Bird entered, carrying a tray of supper
things.

"I don't know about Paddington," said Mrs. Bird. "I've been having enough trouble over the water pipes without missing bears. I think they've got an air lock or something. They've been banging away ever since we came in."

Mr. Brown listened for a moment. "It *does* sound like water pipes," he said. "And yet . . . it isn't regular enough, somehow." He went outside into the hall. "It's a sort of thumping noise. . . ."

"Crikey!" shouted Jonathan. "Listen . . . it's someone sending an S.O.S."

Everyone exchanged glances and then, in one voice cried: "Paddington!"

"Mercy me," said Mrs. Bird as they burst through the papered-up door. "There must have been an earthquake or something. And either that's Paddington or it's his ghost!" She pointed towards a small, white figure as it rose from an upturned bucket to greet them.

"I couldn't find the door," said Paddington, plaintively. "I think I must have papered it over when I did the decorating. It was there when I came in. I remember seeing it. So I banged on the floor with a broom handle."

"Gosh!" said Jonathan, admiringly. "What a mess!"

"You . . . papered . . . it . . . over . . . when . . . you . . . did . . . the . . . decorating," repeated Mr. Brown. He was a bit slow to grasp things sometimes.

"That's right," said Paddington. "I did it as a

162

surprise." He waved a paw round the room. " I'm afraid it's in a bit of a mess, but it isn't dry yet."

While the idea was slowly sinking into Mr. Brown's mind, Mrs. Bird came to Paddington's rescue. " Now it's not a bit of good holding an inquest," she said. " What's done is done. And if you ask me it's a good thing too. Now perhaps we shall get some proper decorators in to do the job." With that she took hold of Paddington's paw and led him out of the room.

" As for you, young bear—you're going straight into a hot bath before all that plaster and stuff sets hard! '

Mr. Brown looked after the retreating figures of Mrs. Bird and Paddington and then at the long trail of white footprints and pawmarks. " Bears! " he said, bitterly.

Paddington hung about in his room for a long time after his bath and waited until the last possible minute before going downstairs to supper. He had a nasty feeling he was in disgrace. But surprisingly the word " decorating " wasn't mentioned at all that evening.

Even more surprisingly, while he was sitting up in bed drinking his cocoa, several people came to see him and each of them gave him sixpence. It was all very mysterious, but Paddington didn't like to ask why in case they changed their minds.

It was Judy who solved the problem for him when she came in to say good night.

" I expect Mummy and Mrs. Bird gave you sixpence because they don't want Daddy to do any more decorat-

ing," she explained. "He always starts things and never finishes them. And I expect Daddy gave you one because he didn't want to finish it anyway. Now they're getting a proper decorator in, so everyone's happy!"

Paddington sipped his cocoa thoughtfully. "Perhaps if I did another room I'd get another one and sixpence," he said.

"Oh, no, you don't," said Judy sternly. "You've done quite enough for one day. If I were you I shouldn't mention the word 'decorating' for a long time to come."

"Perhaps you're right," said Paddington sleepily, as he stretched out his paws. "But I *was* at a loose end."

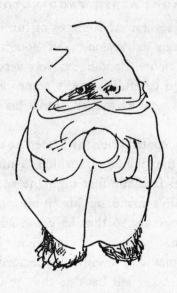

CHAPTER THREE

Paddington Turns Detective

THE OLD BOX-ROOM was finished at last and everyone, including Paddington, agreed that he was a very lucky bear to move into such a nice room. Not only was the paintwork a gleaming white, so that he could almost see his face in it, but the walls were gaily papered and he even had new furniture of his own as well.

"In for a penny, in for a pound!" Mr. Brown had said. And he had bought Paddington a brand new bed with special short legs, a spring mattress, and a cupboard for his odds and ends.

There were several other pieces of furniture and Mrs. Brown had been extravagant and bought a thick pile carpet for the floor. Paddington was very proud of his carpet and he'd carefully spread some old newspapers over the parts where he walked so that his paws wouldn't make it dirty.

Mrs. Bird's contribution had been some bright new curtains for the windows, which Paddington liked very much. In fact, the first night he spent in his new room he couldn't make up his mind whether to have them drawn together so that he could admire them, or left apart so that he could see the view. He got out of bed several times and eventually decided to have one drawn and the other left back so that he could have the best of both worlds.

Then something strange caught his eye. Paddington made a point of keeping a torch by the side of his bed in case there was an emergency during the night, and it was while he was flashing it on and off to admire the drawn curtain that he noticed it. Each time he flashed the torch there was an answering flicker of light from somewhere outside. He sat up in bed, rubbing his eyes, and stared in the direction of the window.

He decided to try a more complicated signal. Two short flashes followed by several long ones. When he did so he nearly fell out of bed with surprise, for each time he sent a signal it was repeated in exactly the same way through the glass.

Paddington jumped out of bed and rushed to the

window. He stayed there for a long while peering out
at the garden, but he couldn't see anything at all. Having
made sure the window was tightly shut, he drew both
curtains and hurried back to bed, pulling the clothes
over his head a little farther than usual. It was all very
mysterious and Paddington didn't believe in taking any
chances.

It was Mr. Brown, at breakfast the next morning,
who gave him his first clue.

"Someone's stolen my prize marrow!" he announced
crossly. "They must have got in during the night."

For some weeks past Mr. Brown had been carefully nursing a huge marrow which he intended to enter for a vegetable show. He watered it morning and evening and measured it every night before going to bed.

Mrs. Brown exchanged a glance with Mrs. Bird. "Never mind, Henry dear," she said. "You've got several others almost as good."

"I *do* mind," grumbled Mr. Brown. "And the others will never be as good—not in time for the show."

"Perhaps it was one of the other competitors, Dad," said Jonathan. "Perhaps they didn't want you to win. It was a jolly good marrow."

"That's quite possible," said Mr. Brown, looking more pleased at the thought. "I've a good mind to offer a small reward."

Mrs. Bird hastily poured out some more tea. Both she and Mrs. Brown appeared anxious to change the subject. But Paddington pricked up his ears at the mention of a reward. As soon as he had finished his toast and marmalade he asked to be excused and disappeared upstairs without even having a third cup of tea.

It was while she was helping Mrs. Bird with the washing-up that Mrs. Brown first noticed something odd going on in the garden.

"Look!" she said, nearly dropping one of the breakfast plates in her astonishment. "Behind the cabbage patch. Whatever is it?"

Mrs. Bird followed her gaze out of the window to

where something brown and shapeless kept bobbing up and down. Her face cleared. "It's Paddington," she said. "I'd recognise his hat anywhere."

"Paddington?" echoed Mrs. Brown. "But what on earth is he doing crawling about in the cabbage patch on his paws and knees?"

"He looks as if he's lost something," said Mrs. Bird. "That's Mr. Brown's magnifying glass he's got."

Mrs. Brown sighed. "Oh, well, we shall know what it is soon enough, I expect."

Unaware of the interest he was causing, Paddington sat down behind a raspberry cane and undid a small notebook which he opened at a page marked LIST OF CLEWS.

Recently Paddington had been reading a mystery story which Mr. Gruber had lent him and he had begun

to fancy himself as a detective. The mysterious flashes of the night before and the loss of Mr. Brown's marrow convinced him his opportunity had come at last.

So far it had all been rather disappointing. He had found several footprints, but he'd traced them all back to the house. In the big gap left by Mr. Brown's prize marrow there were two dead beetles and an empty seed packet, but that was all.

All the same, Paddington wrote the details carefully in his notebook and drew a map of the garden—putting a large X to mark the spot where the marrow had once been. Then he went back upstairs to his room in order to think things out. When he got there he made another addition to his map—a drawing of the new house which was being built beyond the end of the garden. Paddington decided that was where the mysterious flashes must have come from the night before. He stared at it through his opera glasses for some time but the only people he could see were the builders.

Shortly afterwards, anyone watching the Browns' house would have seen the small figure of a bear emerge from the front door and make its way towards the market. Fortunately for Paddington's plans no one saw him leave, nor did anyone see him when he returned some while later carrying a large parcel in his arms. There was an excited gleam in his eyes as he crept back up the stairs and entered his bedroom, carefully locking the door behind him. Paddington liked parcels and this one was particularly interesting.

It took him a long time to undo the knots on the string because his paws were trembling with excitement, but when he did pull the paper apart it revealed a long cardboard box, very brightly coloured, with the words MASTER DETECTIVE'S DISGUISE OUTFIT on the front.

Paddington had been having a battle with himself ever since he'd first seen it several days before in a shop window. Although six shillings seemed an awful lot of money to pay for anything—especially when you only get one and sixpence a week pocket money—Paddington felt very pleased with himself as he emptied the contents on to the floor. There was a long black beard, some dark glasses, a police whistle, several bottles of chemicals marked " Handle with Care "—which Paddington hurriedly put back in the box—a fingerprint pad, a small bottle of invisible ink, and a book of instructions.

It seemed a very good disguise outfit. Paddington tried writing his name on the lid of the box with the invisible ink and he couldn't see it at all. Then he tested the fingerprint pad with his paw and blew several blasts on the police whistle under the bedclothes. He rather wished he'd thought of doing it the other way round as a lot of the ink came off on the sheets, which was going to be difficult to explain.

But he liked the beard best of all. It had two pieces of wire for fitting over the ears, and when he turned and suddenly caught sight of himself in the mirror it quite made him jump. With his hat on, and an old raincoat

of Jonathan's which Mrs. Brown had put out for the
jumble sale, he could hardly recognise himself. After
studying the effect in the mirror from all possible angles,
Paddington decided to try it out downstairs. It was

difficult to walk properly; Jonathan's old coat was too long for him and he kept treading on it. Apart from that, his ears didn't seem to fit the beard as well as he would have liked, so that he had to hang on to it with one paw while he went backwards down the stairs, holding on to the banisters with the other paw. He was so intent on what he was doing that he didn't hear Mrs. Bird coming up until she was right on top of him.

Mrs. Bird looked most startled when she bumped into him. " Oh, Paddington," she began, " I was just coming up to see you. I wonder if you would mind going down to the market for me and fetching half a pound of butter? "

" I'm not Paddington," said a gruff voice from behind the beard. " I'm Sherlock Holmes—the famous detective! "

" Yes, dear," said Mrs. Bird. " But don't forget the butter. We need it for lunch." With that she turned and went back down the stairs towards the kitchen. The door shut behind her and Paddington heard the murmur of voices.

He pulled off the beard disappointedly. " Thirty-six buns worth! " he said bitterly, to no one in particular. He almost felt like going back to the shop and asking for his money back. Thirty-six buns were thirty-six buns and it had taken him a long time to save that much money.

But when he got outside the front door Paddington hesitated. It seemed a pity to waste his disguise, and

even if Mrs. Bird had seen through it, Mr. Briggs, the foreman at the building site, might not. Paddington decided to have one more try. He might even pick up some more clues.

By the time he arrived at the new house he was feeling

much more pleased with himself. Out of the corner of his eye he had noticed quite a number of people staring at him as he passed. And when he'd looked at them over the top of his glasses several of them had hurriedly crossed to the other side of the road.

He crept along outside the house until he heard voices. They seemed to be coming from an open window

on the first floor and he distinctly recognised Mr. Briggs's voice among them. There was a ladder propped against the wall and Paddington clambered up the rungs until his head was level with the window-sill. Then he carefully peered over the edge.

Mr. Briggs and his men were busy round a small stove making themselves a cup of tea. Paddington stared hard at Mr. Briggs, who was in the act of pouring some water into the teapot, and then, after adjusting his beard, he blew a long blast on his police whistle.

There was a crash of breaking china as Mr. Briggs jumped up. He pointed a trembling hand in the direction of the window.

" Cor! " he shouted. " Look! H'an apparition! " The others followed his gaze with open mouths. Paddington stayed just long enough to see four white faces staring at him and then he slid down the ladder on all four paws and hid behind a pile of bricks. Almost immediately there was the sound of excited voices at the window.

" Can't see it now," said a voice. " Must 'ave vanished."

" Cor! " repeated Mr. Briggs, mopping his brow with a spotted handkerchief. " Whatever it was, I don't never want to see nothing like it again. Fair chilled me to the marrow it did! " With that he slammed the window shut and the voices died away.

From behind the pile of bricks Paddington could hardly believe his ears. He had never even dreamed

that Mr. Briggs and his men could be mixed up in the affair. And yet—he had definitely heard Mr. Briggs say his marrow had been chilled.

After removing his beard and dark glasses, Paddington sat down behind the bricks and made several notes in his book with the invisible ink. Then he made his way slowly and thoughtfully in the direction of the grocers.

It had been a very good day's detecting, and Paddington decided he would have to pay another visit to the building site when all was quiet.

It was midnight. All the household had long since gone to bed.

"You know," said Mrs. Brown, just as the clock was striking twelve, "it's a funny thing, but I'm sure Paddington's up to something."

"There's nothing funny in that," replied Mr. Brown, sleepily. "He's always up to *something*. What is it this time?"

"That's just the trouble," said Mrs. Brown. "I don't really know. But he was wandering around wearing a false beard this morning. He nearly startled poor Mrs. Bird out of her wits. He's been writing things in his notebook all the evening too, and do you know what?"

"No," said Mr. Brown, stifling a yawn. "What?"

"When I looked over his shoulder there was nothing there!"

" Oh well, bears will be bears," said Mr. Brown. He paused for a moment as he reached up to turn out the light. " That's strange," he said. " I could have sworn I heard a police whistle just then."

" Nonsense, Henry," said Mrs. Brown. " You must be dreaming."

Mr. Brown shrugged his shoulders as he turned out the light. He was much too tired to argue. All the same he knew he *had* heard a whistle. But as he closed his eyes and prepared himself for sleep, it never crossed his mind that the cause of it might be Paddington.

Lots of things had been happening to Paddington since he'd crept out of the Browns' house under cover of darkness and made his way round to the building site. So many things had happened, one after the other, that he almost wished he'd never decided to be a detective in the first place. He felt very glad when, in answer to several loud blasts on his whistle, a large black car drew up at the side of the road and two men in uniform got out.

" Hallo, hallo," said the first of the men, looking hard at Paddington. " What's going on here? "

Paddington pointed a paw dramatically in the direction of the new house. " I've captured a burglar! " he announced.

" A *what?* " asked the second policeman, peering at Paddington. He'd come across some very strange things in the course of duty, but he'd never been called out in the middle of the night by a young bear before.

This one seemed to be wearing a long black beard and a duffle coat. It was most unusual.

" A burglar," repeated Paddington. " I think he's the one that took Mr. Brown's marrow! "

" Mr. Brown's marrow? " repeated the first police-

man, looking rather dazed as he followed Paddington through his secret entrance into the house.

" That's right," said Paddington. " Now he's got my marmalade sandwiches. I took a big parcel of them inside with me in case I got hungry while I was waiting."

" Of course," said the second policeman, trying to

humour Paddington. "Marmalade sandwiches." He tapped his forehead as he looked at his colleague. "And where is the burglar now—eating your sandwiches?"

"I expect so," said Paddington. "I shut him in the room and I put a piece of wood under the door so that he couldn't get out. I got my beard caught in one of the sandwiches—so I switched my torch on to take some of the hairs out of the marmalade and then it happened!"

"*What* happened?" chorused the policemen. They were finding it rather difficult to keep up with Paddington's description of the course of events.

"I saw someone flashing a light outside the window," explained Paddington, as patiently as he could. "Then I heard footsteps coming up the stairs, so I lay in wait." He pointed towards a door at the top of the stairs. "He's in there!"

Before either of the policemen could ask any more questions there came the sound of banging and a voice cried, "Let me out!"

"Good heavens!" exclaimed the first policeman. "There *is* someone in there!" He looked at Paddington with renewed respect. "Did you get a description, sir?"

"He was about eight feet tall," said Paddington, recklessly, "and he sounded very cross when he found he couldn't get out."

"Hmm!" said the second policeman. "Well, we'll soon see about that. Stand back!" With that he pulled

the piece of wood from under the door and flung it open, shining his torch into the room.

Everyone stood back and waited for the worst to happen. To their surprise, when the man came out it was another policeman.

" Locked in! " he exclaimed, bitterly. " I see some lights flashing from an empty house, so I go to investigate . . . and what happens? I'm locked in . . . by a *bear*! " He pointed towards Paddington. " And if I'm not mistaken, that's him! "

Paddington suddenly began to feel very small. All three policemen were looking at him, and in the excitement his beard had fallen off one ear.

" Hmm," said the first policeman. " And what were *you* doing in an empty house at gone midnight, young fellow me bear? And wearing a disguise at that! I can see we shall have to take you along to the station for questioning."

" It's a bit difficult to explain," said Paddington, sadly. " I'm afraid it's going to take rather a long time. You see . . . it's all to do with Mr. Brown's marrow— the one he was going to enter for the vegetable show . . ."

The policemen weren't the only ones who found it all rather hard to understand. Mr. Brown was still asking questions long after Paddington had been returned from the police station to their safe keeping.

" I still don't see how my losing a marrow has got anything to do with Paddington being arrested," he said for the hundredth time.

"But Paddington wasn't arrested, Henry," said Mrs. Brown. "He was only detained for questioning. Anyway, he was only trying to get your marrow back for you. You ought to be very grateful."

She sighed. She would have to tell her husband the truth sooner or later. She'd already told Paddington. "I'm afraid it's all my fault really," she said. "You see . . . *I* cut your marrow by mistake!"

"*You* did?" exclaimed Mr. Brown. "You cut my prize marrow?"

"Well, I didn't realise it was your prize one," said Mrs. Brown. "And you know how fond you are of stuffed marrow. We had it for dinner last night!"

Back in his own room, Paddington felt quite pleased with himself as he got into bed. He'd have a lot to tell his friend, Mr. Gruber, in the morning. Once the inspector at the police station had heard his full story he had complimented Paddington on his bravery and ordered his immediate release.

"I wish there were more bears about like you, Mr. Brown," he had said. And he had given Paddington a real police whistle as a souvenir. Even the policeman who had been locked in said he quite understood how it had all come about.

Besides, he had solved the mystery of the flashing lights at last. It hadn't been anyone in the garden at all, but simply the reflection of his own torch on the window. When he stood up on the end of the bed he could even see himself quite plainly in the glass.

In a way Paddington was sorry about the marrow. Especially as he wouldn't get the reward. But he was very glad the culprit hadn't been Mr. Briggs. He liked Mr. Briggs—and besides, he'd been promised another ride in his bucket. He didn't want to miss that.

CHAPTER FOUR

Paddington and the Bonfire

SOON AFTER the marrow adventure the weather changed.
It began to get colder. The leaves fell from the trees
and it became dark very early in the evenings. Jonathan
and Judy went back to school and Paddington was left
on his own for much of the day.

But one morning, towards the end of October, a letter
arrived with his name on the envelope. It was marked
"Urgent" and "Strictly Personal" and it was in
Jonathan's writing. Paddington didn't get many letters,

only an occasional picture postcard from his Aunt Lucy in Peru, so it was all the more exciting.

In some ways it was a rather mysterious letter and Paddington couldn't make head or tail of it. In it Jonathan asked him to collect all the dry leaves he could find and sweep them into a pile ready for when he came home in a few days' time. Paddington puzzled about it for a long time, and in the end he decided to consult his friend Mr. Gruber on the subject. Mr. Gruber knew about most things, and even if he couldn't tell the answer to a question straight away, he had a huge library of books in his antique shop and knew just where to look. He and Paddington often had a long chat about things in general over their morning cocoa, and Mr. Gruber liked nothing better than to help Paddington with his problems.

" A problem shared is a problem halved, Mr. Brown," he was fond of saying. "And I must say, that since you came to live in the district I've never been short of things to look up."

As soon as he had finished his breakfast, Paddington put on his scarf and duffle coat, collected the morning shopping list from Mrs. Bird, and set off with his basket on wheels towards the shops in the Portobello Road.

Paddington enjoyed shopping. He was a popular bear with the street traders in the market, even though he usually struck a hard bargain. He always compared the prices on the various stalls very carefully before

actually buying anything. Mrs. Bird said he made the housekeeping money go twice as far as anyone else.

It was even colder outside than Paddington had expected, and when he stopped to look in a newsagent's on the way, his breath made the bottom of the window quite cloudy. Paddington was a polite bear, and when he saw the shopkeeper glaring at him through the door he carefully rubbed the steamy part with his paw in case anyone else wanted to look in. As he did so he suddenly noticed that the inside of the window had changed since he'd last passed that way.

Before, it had been full of chocolate and sweets. Now they were all gone and in their place was a very ragged-looking dummy sitting on top of a pile of logs. It held a notice in its hand which said:

REMEMBER, REMEMBER, THE FIFTH OF NOVEMBER,
GUNPOWDER, TREASON AND PLOT.

And underneath that was an even larger notice saying:

GET YOUR FIREWORKS HERE!

Paddington studied it all carefully for a few moments and then hurried on to Mr. Gruber's, pausing only to pick up his morning supply of buns at the bakery, where he had a standing order.

Now that the cold weather had set in, Mr. Gruber no longer sat on the pavement in front of his shop in the morning. Instead, he had arranged a sofa by the stove in the back of the shop. It was a cosy corner,

surrounded by books, but Paddington didn't like it quite
so much as being outside. For one thing, the sofa was
an old one and some of the horsehairs poked through,
but he quickly forgot about this as he handed Mr.
Gruber his share of buns and began telling him of the
morning's happenings.

"Gunpowder, treason and plot?" said Mr. Gruber,
as he handed Paddington a large mug of steaming cocoa.
"Why, that's to do with Guy Fawkes' day."

He smiled apologetically and rubbed the steam from
his glasses when he saw that Paddington still looked
puzzled.

"I always forget, Mr. Brown," he said, "that you

come from Darkest Peru. I don't suppose you know about Guy Fawkes."

Paddington wiped the cocoa from his whiskers with the back of his paw in case it left a stain and shook his head.

"Well," continued Mr. Gruber. "I expect you've seen fireworks before. I seem to remember when I was in South America many years ago they always had them on fête days."

Paddington nodded. Now that Mr. Gruber mentioned it, he did remember his Aunt Lucy taking him to a firework display. Although he'd only been very small at the time he had enjoyed it very much.

"We only have fireworks once a year here," said Mr. Gruber. "On November the Fifth." And then he went on to tell Paddington all about the plot to blow up the Houses of Parliament many years ago, and how its discovery at the last moment had been celebrated ever since by the burning of bonfires and letting off of fireworks.

Mr. Gruber was very good at explaining things and Paddington thanked him when he had finished.

Mr. Gruber sighed and a far away look came into his eyes. "It's a long time since I had any fireworks of my own, Mr. Brown," he said. "A very long time indeed."

"Well, Mr. Gruber," said Paddington, importantly. "I think we're going to have a display. You must come to ours."

Mr. Gruber looked so pleased at being invited that Paddington hurried off at once to finish his shopping. He was anxious to get back to the newsagent's quickly so that he could investigate the fireworks properly.

When he entered the shop the man looked at him doubtfully over the top of the counter. " Fireworks? " he said. " I'm not sure that I'm supposed to serve young bears with fireworks."

Paddington gave him a hard stare. " In Darkest Peru," he said, remembering all that Mr. Gruber had told him, "we had fireworks every fête day."

" I dare say," said the man. " But this isn't Darkest Peru—nor nothing like it. What do you want—bangers or the other sort? "

" I think I'd like to try some you can hold in the paw for a start," said Paddington.

The man hesitated. " All right," he said. " I'll etl you have a packet of best sparklers. But if you singe your whiskers don't come running to me grumbling and wanting your money back."

Paddington promised he would be very careful and was soon hurrying back up the road towards the Browns' house. As he rounded the last corner he bumped into a small boy wheeling a pram.

The boy held out a cap containing several coppers and touched his hat respectfully. " Penny for the Guy, sir."

" Thank you very much," said Paddington, taking a penny out of the cap. " It's very kind of you."

"Oi!" said the boy as Paddington turned to go.
"Oi! You're supposed to give *me* a penny—not take
one yourself."

Paddington stared at him. "Give *you* a penny?"
he said, hardly able to believe his ears. "What for?"

"For the Guy, of course," said the boy. "That's
what I said—a penny for the Guy!" He pointed to the
pram and Paddington noticed for the first time that there
was a figure inside it. It was dressed in an old suit and
wearing a mask. It looked just like the one he'd seen
in the shop window earlier that morning.

Paddington was so surprised that he had undone his
suitcase and placed a penny in the boy's hat before he
really knew what he was doing.

"If you don't like giving a penny for the Guy," said
the small boy as he turned to go, " why don't you get

one of your own? All you need is an old suit and a bit of straw."

Paddington was very thoughtful as he made his way home. He even almost forgot to ask for a second helping at lunch.

" I do hope he hasn't hit on another of his ideas," said Mrs. Brown, as Paddington asked to be excused and disappeared into the garden. " It's most unlike him to have to be reminded about things like that. Especially when it's stew. He's usually so fond of dumplings."

" I expect it is an Idea," said Mrs. Bird, ominously. " I know the signs."

" Well, I expect the fresh air will do him good," said Mrs. Brown, looking out of the window. " And it's very good of him to offer to sweep up all the leaves. The garden's in such a mess."

" It's November," said Mrs. Bird. "Guy Fawkes!"

" Oh! " said Mrs. Brown. " *Oh dear!* "

For the next hour Paddington enjoyed himself in the garden with Mrs. Bird's dustpan and brush. The Browns had a number of trees and very soon he had a large pile of leaves, almost twice his own height, in the middle of the cabbage patch. It was while he was sitting down for a rest in the middle of a flower bed that he felt someone watching him.

He looked up to see Mr. Curry, the Browns' next door neighbour, eyeing him suspiciously over the fence. Mr. Curry wasn't very fond of bears and he was always

trying to catch Paddington doing something he shouldn't so that he could report him. He had a reputation in the neighbourhood for being mean and disagreeable, and the Browns had as little to do with him as possible.

" What are you doing, bear? " he growled at Paddington. " I hope you're not thinking of setting light to all those leaves."

" Oh, no," said Paddington. " It's for Guy Fawkes."

" Fireworks! " said Mr. Curry, grumpily. " Nasty things. Banging away and frightening people."

Paddington, who had been toying with the idea of trying out one of his sparklers, hastily hid the packet behind his back. " Aren't you having any fireworks then, Mr. Curry? " he asked, politely.

" Fireworks? " Mr. Curry looked at Paddington with distaste. " Me? I can't afford them, bear. Waste of money. And what's more, if I get any coming over in *my* garden I shall report the whole matter to the police! "

Paddington felt very glad he hadn't tested his sparkler.

" Mind you, bear "—a sly gleam came into Mr. Curry's eye and he looked round carefully to make sure no one else was listening—" if anyone likes to invite me to their firework display, that's a different matter." He signalled Paddington over to the fence and began whispering in his ear. As Paddington listened his face got longer and longer and his whiskers began to sag.

" I think it's disgraceful," said Mrs. Bird later on that day when she heard that Mr. Curry had invited

himself to the firework party. "Frightening a young
bear like that with talk of police and such like. Just
because he's too mean to buy his own fireworks. It's
a good job he didn't say it to me—I'd have told him a
thing or two!"

"Poor Paddington," said Mrs. Brown. "He looked
most upset. Where is he now?"

"I don't know," said Mrs. Bird. "He's gone off
somewhere looking for some straw. I expect it's to do
with his bonfire."

She returned to the subject of Mr. Curry. "When I
think of all the errands that young bear's run for him—
wearing his paws to the bone—just because he's too
lazy to go himself."

"He does take advantage of people," said Mrs.
Brown. "Why, he even left his old suit on the porch
this morning to be collected by our laundry for cleaning."

"Did he?" exclaimed Mrs. Bird, grimly. "Well,
we'll soon see about *that*!" She hurried out to the front
door and then called out to Mrs. Brown. "You *did* say
the porch?"

"That's right," replied Mrs. Brown. "In the corner."

"It's not there now," called Mrs. Bird. "Someone
must have taken it away."

"That's very strange," said Mrs. Brown. "I didn't
hear anyone knock. And the laundryman hasn't been
yet. How very odd."

"It'll serve him right," said Mrs. Bird, as she

returned to the kitchen, " if someone's taken it. That'll teach him a lesson! " In spite of her stern appearance, Mrs. Bird was a kindly soul at heart, but she became very cross when people took advantage of others, especially Paddington.

" Oh well," said Mrs. Brown. " I expect it'll sort itself out. I must try and remember to ask Paddington if he's seen it when he comes in."

As it happened Paddington was gone for quite a long time, so that when he did finally return, Mrs. Brown had forgotten all about the matter. It had been dark for some time when he let himself into the garden by the back way. He pushed his basket up the path until he reached Mr. Brown's shed, and then, after a struggle, managed to lift a large object out of the basket, and place it in a corner behind the lawn-mower. There was also a small cardboard box marked GI FAWKS, which rattled when he shook it.

Paddington shut the door of the shed, carefully hid the cardboard box underneath his hat in the bottom of the basket, and then crept quietly out of the garden and round to the front door. He felt pleased with himself. It had been a very good evening's work indeed—much better than he had expected—and that night, before he went to sleep, he spent a long time writing a letter to Jonathan in which he told him all about it.

" Gosh, Paddington," exclaimed Jonathan, several days later, when they were getting ready for the display.

" What a super lot of fireworks! " He peered into the cardboard box, which was full almost to the brim. " I've never seen so many."

" Honestly, Paddington," said Judy, admiringly. " Anyone would think you'd been collecting in the street or something."

Paddington waved a paw vaguely through the air and exchanged a knowing glance with Jonathan. But before he had time to explain things to Judy, Mr. Brown entered the room.

He was dressed in an overcoat and gumboots and he was carrying a lighted candle. " Right," he said. " Are we all ready? Mr. Gruber's waiting in the hall and Mrs. Bird's got the chairs all ready on the veranda." Mr. Brown looked as eager as anyone to start the firework display and he eyed Paddington's box enviously.

" I vote," he said, holding up his hand for silence when they were all outside in the garden, " that as this is Paddington's first November the Fifth, we let him set off the first firework."

" Hear! Hear! " applauded Mr. Gruber. " What sort would you like, Mr. Brown?"

Paddington looked thoughtfully at the box. There were so many different shapes and sizes it was difficult to decide.

194

" I think I'll have one of those you can hold in the paw first," he said. " I think I'll have a sparkler."

" Dull things, sparklers," said Mr. Curry, who was sitting in the best chair helping himself to some marmalade sandwiches.

" If Paddington wants a sparkler, he shall have one," said Mrs. Bird, giving Mr. Curry a freezing look.

Mr. Brown handed Paddington the candle, taking care not to let the hot fat drip on to his fur, and there was a round of applause as the sparkler burst into life. Paddington waved it over his head several times and there was another round of applause as he moved it up and down to spell out the letters P-A-D-I-N-G-T-U-N.

" Very effective," said Mr. Gruber.

" But that's not how you spell *Paddington*," grumbled Mr. Curry, his mouth full of sandwich.

" It's how *I* spell it," said Paddington. He gave Mr. Curry one of his special hard stares, but unfortunately it was dark and so the full effect was lost.

" How about lighting the bonfire? " said Mr. Brown hurriedly. " Then we can all see what we're doing." There was a crackle from the dried leaves as he bent down to apply the match.

" That's better," said Mr. Curry, rubbing his hands together. " I find it rather draughty on this veranda of yours. I think I'll let off a few more fireworks if there are no more sandwiches left." He looked across at Mrs. Bird.

" There aren't," said Mrs. Bird. " You've just had

195

the last one. Honestly," she continued, as Mr. Curry moved away and began rummaging in Paddington's box. " The cheek of some people. And he never even brought so much as a Catherine Wheel himself."

" He does spoil things," said Mrs. Brown. " Everyone's been looking forward to this evening. I've a good mind . . ." Whatever Mrs. Brown had been about to say was lost as there came a cry from the direction of the garden shed.

" Crikey, Paddington," shouted Jonathan. " Why ever didn't you tell us? "

" Tell us what? " asked Mr. Brown, trying to divide his attention between a Roman Candle which had just fizzled out and the mysterious object which Jonathan was dragging from the shed.

" It's a Guy! " shouted Judy with delight.

" It's a super one too! " exclaimed Jonathan. " It looks just like a real person. Is it yours, Paddington? "

" Well," said Paddington, " yes . . . and no." He looked rather worried. In the excitement he had quite forgotten about the Guy which he'd used when he'd collected the money for the fireworks. He wasn't at all sure he wanted the others to know about it in case too many questions were asked.

" A Guy? " said Mr. Curry. " Then it had better go on the bonfire." He peered at it through the smoke. For some odd reason there was a familiar look about it which he couldn't quite place.

" Oh, no," said Paddington, hurriedly. " I don't

think you'd better do that. It's not really for burning."

"Nonsense, bear," said Mr. Curry. "I can see you don't know much about Guy Fawkes' night. Guys are always burned." He pushed the others on one side and with the help of Mr. Brown's garden rake placed the Guy on top of the bonfire.

"There!" he exclaimed, as he stood back rubbing his hands. "That's better. That's what I call a bonfire."

Mr. Brown removed his glasses, polished them, and then looked hard at the bonfire. He didn't recognise the suit the Guy was wearing and he was glad to see it wasn't one of his. All the same, he had a nasty feeling at the back of his mind. "It . . . it seems a very well dressed sort of Guy," he remarked.

Mr. Curry started and then stepped forward to take a closer look. Now that the bonfire was well and truly alight it was easier to see. The trousers were blazing merrily and the jacket had just started to smoulder. His eyes nearly popped out and he pointed a trembling finger towards the flames.

"That's my suit!" he roared. "My suit! The one you were supposed to send to the cleaners!"

"What!" exclaimed Mr. Brown. Everyone turned to look at Paddington.

Paddington was as surprised as the others. It was the first he had heard of Mr. Curry's suit. "I found it on the doorstep," he said. "I thought it had been put out for the rummage sale. . . ."

"The *rummage sale?*" cried Mr. Curry, almost

beside himself with rage. "The *rummage sale*? My best suit! I'll . . .I'll . . ." Mr. Curry was spluttering so much he couldn't think of anything to say. But Mrs. Bird could.

"To start with," she said, "it wasn't your best suit. It's been sent to the cleaners at least six times to my knowledge. And I'm quite sure Paddington didn't know it was yours. In any case," she finished triumphantly, "who was it insisted it should go on the bonfire in the first place?"

Mr. Brown tried hard not to laugh, and then he caught Mr. Gruber's eye looking at him over the top of his handkerchief. "You *did*, you know," he spluttered. "You said put it on the bonfire. And Paddington tried to stop you!"

Mr. Curry struggled hard for a moment as he looked from one to the other. But he knew when he was beaten. He gave one final glare all round the party and then slammed the door behind him.

"Well," chuckled Mr. Gruber, "I must say that when young Mr. Brown's around there's never a dull moment!" He felt underneath his chair and brought out a cardboard box. "Now I vote we get on with the display. And just in case we run out of fireworks—I've brought a few more along."

"You know, it's funny you should say that," said Mr. Brown, feeling under *his* chair. "But I have some as well!"

Afterwards everyone in the neighbourhood voted it

was the best firework display they had seen for many a year. Quite a number of people turned up to watch, and even Mr. Curry was seen peeping from behind his curtains on several occasions.

And as Paddington lifted a tired paw and waved the last sparkler in the air to spell out the words T-H-E E-N-D, everyone agreed they had never seen such a successful bonfire before—or such a well-dressed Guy.

CHAPTER FIVE

Trouble at Number Thirty-two

THAT EVENING, after the bonfire had died away, the weather suddenly became even colder. When Paddington went upstairs to bed he opened his window a few inches and peeped out in case there were any more fireworks to see. He sniffed the cold night air and then hastily shut the window, diving into bed and pulling the blankets over his ears.

In the morning he woke much earlier than usual, shivering with the cold, and found to his surprise that the ends of his whiskers, which had become uncovered

during the night, were quite stiff. Having listened for a while to make sure breakfast was being cooked, he put on his duffle coat and went along to the bathroom.

When he reached the bathroom, Paddington made several interesting discoveries. First, his flannel, which he'd left folded over the towel rail the night before, was as stiff as a board, and it made a funny cracking noise when he tried to bend it straight. Then, when he turned the tap, nothing happened. Paddington decided quite quickly that he wasn't meant to wash that morning and hurried back to his own room.

But when he got there he had yet another surprise. He drew the curtains and tried to look out of his window, only to find that it was all white and frosted—just like the one in the bathroom. Paddington breathed heavily on the glass and rubbed it with the back of his paw. When he had made a hole big enough to peer through, he nearly fell over backwards with astonishment.

All traces of the previous evening's bonfire had completely vanished. Instead, everything was covered by a thick blanket of white. Not only that, but there were millions of large white flakes falling out of the sky.

He rushed downstairs to tell the others. The Browns were all sitting round the breakfast table when he burst into the dining-room. Paddington waved his paws wildly in the air and called for them to look out of the window.

" Good heavens! " exclaimed Mr. Brown, looking up from his morning paper. " What *is* the matter? "

"Look!" said Paddington, pointing towards the garden. "Everything's gone white!"

Judy threw back her head and laughed. "It's all right, Paddington—it's only snow. It happens every year."

"Snow?" said Paddington, looking puzzled. "What's snow?"

"It's a nuisance," said Mr. Brown, crossly. Mr. Brown wasn't in a very good mood that morning. He hadn't expected the weather to change so quickly and all the upstairs water pipes had frozen. To make matters worse, everyone had been blaming him because he'd forgotten to stoke the boiler before going to bed.

"Snow?" said Judy. "Well, it's . . it's sort of frozen rain. It's very soft."

"Jolly good for snowballs," exclaimed Jonathan. "We'll show you how to make them after breakfast. We can clear the paths at the same time."

Paddington sat down at the breakfast table and began undoing his napkin, hardly able to take his eyes off the scene outside the window.

"Paddington!" said Mrs. Brown, suspiciously. "Did you wear your duffle coat when you washed this morning?"

"A lick and a promise," said Mrs. Bird, as she handed him a steaming bowl of porridge. "And more promise than lick if you ask me."

But Paddington was much too busy thinking about the snow to hear what they were saying. He was wonder-

ing if he could speed up the breakfast by having all his things on the one plate. But just as he reached out for the bacon and eggs and the marmalade, he caught Mrs. Bird's eye and hurriedly pretended he was only conducting to the music on the wireless.

"If you do go out after breakfast, Paddington," said Mrs. Brown, "I think it would be nice if you could clear Mr. Curry's path for him before you do ours. We all know it wasn't your fault about his suit last night, but it would show you mean well."

"That's a good idea," exclaimed Jonathan. "We'll give you a hand. Then we can use all the snow we get to build a snowman this afternoon. How about it, Paddington?"

Paddington looked rather doubtful. Whenever he tried to do anything for Mr. Curry, something always seemed to go wrong.

"But no playing snowballs," warned Mrs. Bird. "Mr. Curry always sleeps with his bedroom window open—even in the middle of winter. If you wake him he won't like it at all."

Paddington, Jonathan and Judy agreed to be as quiet as they could and as soon as breakfast was over they dressed in their warmest clothes and rushed outside to look at the snow.

Paddington was very impressed. It was much deeper than he had expected, but not at all as cold as he thought it would be, except when he stood for very long in the one place. Within a few minutes all three were busy

with shovels and brooms clearing Mr. Curry's paths for
him.

Jonathan and Judy started on the pavement outside
the house. Paddington fetched his seaside bucket and
spade and began work on Mr. Curry's back garden path,
which was not quite so wide.

He filled his bucket with snow and then tipped it
through a hole in the Browns' fence near the place
they intended building a snowman later in the day. It
was hard work, for the snow was deep and came right
up to the edge of his duffle coat, and as fast as he cleared
a space, more snow came down, covering the part he'd
just done.

After working for what seemed like hours, Paddington decided to have a rest. But no sooner had he settled
himself on the bucket than something hit him on the
back of the head, nearly knocking his hat off into the
bargain.

" Caught you! " yelled Jonathan with delight. " Come
on, Paddington—make yourself some snowballs—then
we can have a fight."

Paddington jumped up from his bucket and dodged
round the side of Mr. Curry's shed. Then, after first
making sure Mrs. Bird was nowhere in sight, he gathered
up some snow and rolled it into a hard ball. Holding it
firmly in his right paw he closed his eyes and took
careful aim.

" Yah! " shouted Jonathan, as Paddington opened his
eyes. " Missed me by a mile. You'd better get some
practise in! "

Paddington stood behind Mr. Curry's shed scratching his head and examining his paw. He knew the snowball must have gone somewhere but he hadn't the least idea where. After thinking about it for some time he decided to have another go. If he crept very quietly round the side of the house he might even be able to catch Jonathan unawares and get his own back.

It was as he tip-toed past Mr. Curry's back door, clutching a snowball in his paw, that he noticed for the first time the door was open. The wind was blowing the snow through into the kitchen and there was already a small pile of it on the mat. Paddington hesitated for a moment and then pulled the door shut. There was a click as it closed, and he carefully tested it with his paw to make certain it was properly fastened. He was sure Mr. Curry wouldn't want snow all over his kitchen floor, and he felt very pleased at being able to do another good deed—apart from sweeping the path.

To Paddington's surprise, when he peered round the corner at the front of the house Mr. Curry was already there. He was wearing a dressing gown over his pyjamas and he looked cold and cross. He broke off his conversation with Jonathan and Judy and stared in Paddington's direction.

" Ah, there you are, bear! " he exclaimed. " Have you been throwing snowballs? "

" Snowballs? " repeated Paddington, hurriedly putting his paw behind his back. " Did you say snowballs, Mr. Curry? "

"Yes," said Mr. Curry. "*Snowballs!* A large one
came through my bedroom window a moment ago and
landed right in the middle of my bed. Now it's all
melted on my hot-water bottle! If I thought you had
done it on purpose, bear . . ."

"Oh no, Mr. Curry," said Paddington, earnestly.
"I wouldn't do a thing like that *on purpose*. I don't
think I could. It's difficult throwing snowballs by paw—
especially big ones like that."

"Like what?" asked Mr. Curry, suspiciously.

"Like the one you said landed in your bed," said

Paddington, sounding rather confused. He was beginning to wish Mr. Curry would hurry up and go. The snowball was making his paw very cold.

" Mmm," said Mr. Curry. " Well I'm not standing out here in the snow discussing bears' pranks. I came downstairs intending to tell you off." He looked round approvingly at the clean pavement. " But I must admit I've been pleasantly surprised. In fact," he turned to go back indoors, " if you make as good a job of the rest I might even give you a penny! "

" Between you," he added, in case they mistook his meaning.

" A penny! " exclaimed Jonathan, disgustedly. " One measly penny."

" Oh, well," said Judy, " at least we've done our good deed for the day. It should last for a while—even with Mr. Curry."

Paddington looked doubtful. " I don't think it'll last *very* long," he said, listening hard. " In fact, I think it's nearly over." Even as he spoke there came a roar of rage from Mr. Curry followed by several loud bangs.

" Whatever's up now? " exclaimed Judy. " That sounds like Mr. Curry banging on his back door."

" I thought I was doing him a good turn," said Paddington, looking very worried, " so I shut it. I think he must be locked out."

" Oh gosh, Paddington," groaned Judy. " You are an unlucky bear to-day."

"Who shut my door?" roared Mr. Curry, as he strode round to the front again. "Who locked me out of my house? Bear!" he barked. "Where are you, bear?"

Mr. Curry glared down the road but there was not a soul in sight. If he had been a little less cross, he might have noticed three distinct sets of paw- and footprints where Paddington, Jonathan and Judy had beaten a hasty retreat.

After a distance the three tracks separated. Jonathan's and Judy's disappeared into the Browns' house. Paddington's went towards the market.

He had seen quite enough of Mr. Curry for one day. Besides, it had gone half-past ten and he had promised to meet Mr. Gruber for morning cocoa at eleven.

"I really think Mr. Curry has gone a bit funny in the head," said Mrs. Brown, later that day. "He was standing outside the house in his pyjamas and dressing gown this morning—in all that snow. Then he started running around in circles waving his fist."

"Mmm," replied Mrs. Bird. "I saw Paddington playing snowballs in his back garden just before that happened."

"Oh dear," said Mrs. Brown. She looked out of the window. The sky had cleared at last and the garden, with all the trees bowed down under the weight of snow, looked just like a Christmas card. "It seems very still," she said. "Almost as if something was about to happen."

Mrs. Bird followed her gaze. "They've made a wonderful snowman. I've never seen quite such a good one before. It's only small but it looks most lifelike."

"Isn't that Paddington's old hat they've put on top?" asked Mrs. Brown. She looked round as the door opened and Jonathan and Judy entered the room. "We were just saying," she continued. "What a lovely snowman you've made."

"It isn't a snowman," said Jonathan, mysteriously. "It's a snow*bear*. It's meant to be a surprise for Dad. He's coming down the road now."

"It looks as if he'll have more than one surprise coming his way," said Mrs. Bird. "I can see Mr. Curry waiting for him by the fence."

"Oh, crikey!" groaned Jonathan. "That's torn it."

"Trust Mr. Curry to spoil things," said Judy. "I hope he doesn't keep Dad talking too long."

"Why, dear?" asked Mrs. Brown. "Does it matter?"

"Does it *matter*?" cried Jonathan, rushing to the window. "I'll say it does!"

Mrs. Brown didn't pursue the subject. She had no doubt that she would hear all about it in due course— whatever it was.

It took Mr. Brown a long time to get rid of Mr. Curry and put his car away in the garage. When he did come indoors he looked very fed up.

"That Mr. Curry," he exclaimed. "Telling tales about Paddington again. If I'd been there this morning

he'd have got more than a snowball in his bed." He
looked round the room. " By the way, where *is* Paddington?" Paddington usually liked helping Mr. Brown
put his car away and it was most unusual for him not
to be there ready to give paw signals.

" I haven't seen him for ages," said Mrs. Brown.
She looked at Jonathan and Judy. " Do *you* know where
he is?"

" Didn't he jump out at you, Dad?" asked Jonathan.

" Jump out at me?" exclaimed Mr. Brown, looking
puzzled. " Not that I know of. Why, was he supposed
to?"

" But you saw the snowbear, didn't you?" asked Judy.
" Just by the garage."

" Snow*bear*?" said Mr. Brown. " Good heavens—
you don't mean—that wasn't Paddington?"

" What's that young bear been up to now?" asked
Mrs. Bird. " Do you mean to say he's been out there
covered in snow all this time? I've never heard of such
a thing."

" Well, it wasn't really his idea," said Jonathan. " Not
all of it."

" I expect he heard Mr. Curry's voice and got
frightened." said Judy.

" Just you bring him indoors at once," said Mrs.
Bird. " Why, he might catch his death of cold. I've a
good mind to send him to bed without any supper."

It wasn't that Mrs. Bird was cross with Paddington—
she **was** simply worried in case anything happened to

him, and when he came through the door her manner changed at once.

She took one of his paws in her hand and then felt his nose. " Good gracious! " she exclaimed. " He's like an iceberg."

Paddington shivered. " I don't think I like being a snowbear very much," he said, in a weak voice.

" I should think not indeed," exclaimed Mrs. Bird. She turned to the others. " That bear's going to bed at once—with a hot-water bottle and a bowl of broth. Then I'm sending for the doctor."

With that she made Paddington sit by the fire while she hurried upstairs to fetch a thermometer.

Paddington lay back in Mr. Brown's armchair with his eyes closed. He certainly felt very strange. He couldn't remember ever having felt like it before. One moment he seemed to be as cold as the snow outside, the next he felt as if he was on fire.

He wasn't quite sure how long he lay there, but he vaguely remembered Mrs. Bird sticking something long and cold under his tongue, which she told him not to bite. After that he didn't remember much more, except that everyone started running around, preparing soup and filling hot-water bottles, and generally making sure his room was comfortable for him.

Within a few minutes everything was ready and the Browns all trooped upstairs to make sure he was properly tucked in bed. Paddington thanked them all very much

and then, after waving a paw limply in their direction, lay back and closed his eyes.

"He *must* be feeling bad," whispered Mrs. Bird. "He hasn't even touched his soup."

"Gosh," said Jonathan, miserably, as he followed Judy down the stairs. "It was mostly my idea. I shall never forgive myself if anything happens to him."

"It was my idea as well," said Judy, comfortingly. "I expect we all thought of it together. Anyway," she added, as the front door bell rang, "that must be the doctor—so we shall soon know."

Doctor MacAndrew was a long time with Paddington, and when he came downstairs again he looked very serious.

"How is he, Doctor?" asked Mrs. Brown, anxiously. "He's not seriously ill, is he?"

"Aye, he is," said Doctor MacAndrew. "Ye may as well know. That young bear's verra ill indeed. Playing in the snow when he's not used to it no doubt. I've given him a wee drop o' medicine to tide him over the night and I'll be along first thing in the morning."

"But he *is* going to be all right, isn't he, Doctor MacAndrew?" cried Judy.

Doctor MacAndrew shook his head gravely. "I wouldna care to give an opinion," he said. "I wouldna care to give an opinion at all." With that he bade them all good-night and drove away.

It was a very sad party of Browns that went upstairs

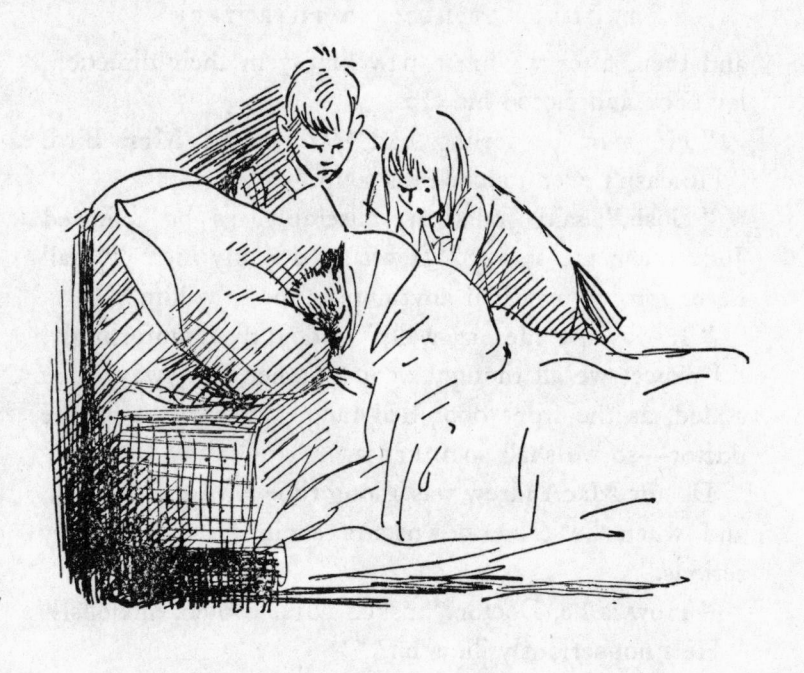

that evening. While they were getting ready for bed,
Mrs. Bird quietly moved her things into Paddington's
room so that she could keep an eye on him during the
night.

But she wasn't the only one who couldn't think of
sleep. Several times the door to Paddington's room
gently opened and either Mr. and Mrs. Brown or Jonathan and Judy crept in to see how he was getting on.
Somehow it didn't seem possible that anything *could*
happen to Paddington. But every time they looked at
Mrs. Bird she just shook her head and went on with her
sewing so that they couldn't see her face.

The next day the news of Paddington's illness quickly spread around the neighbourhood and by lunch time there was a steady stream of callers asking after him.

Mr. Gruber was the first on the scene. " I wondered what had happened to young Mr. Brown when he didn't turn up for elevenses this morning," he said, looking very upset. " I kept his cocoa hot for over an hour."

Mr. Gruber went away again, but returned shortly afterwards carrying a bunch of grapes and a large basket of fruit and flowers from the rest of the traders in the Portobello market. " I'm afraid there isn't much about at this time of the year," he said apologetically. " But we've done the best we can."

He paused at the door. " I'm sure he'll be all right, Mrs. Brown," he said. " With so many people *wanting* him to get well, I'm sure he will."

Mr. Gruber raised his hat to Mrs. Brown and then began walking slowly in the direction of the park. Somehow he didn't want to go back to his shop that day.

Even Mr. Curry knocked on the door that afternoon and brought with him an apple and a jar of calves' foot jelly, which he said was very good for invalids.

Mrs. Bird took all the presents up to Paddington's room and placed them carefully beside his bed in case he should wake up and want something to eat.

Doctor MacAndrew called a number of times during the next two days, but despite everything he did, there

seemed to be no change at all. " We'll just have to bide our time," was all he would say.

It was three days later, at breakfast time, that the door to the Browns' dining-room burst open and Mrs. Bird rushed in.

" Oh, do come quickly," she cried. " It's Paddington! "

Everyone jumped up from the table and stared at Mrs. Bird.

" He's . . . he's not worse, is he? " asked Mrs. Brown, voicing the thoughts of them all.

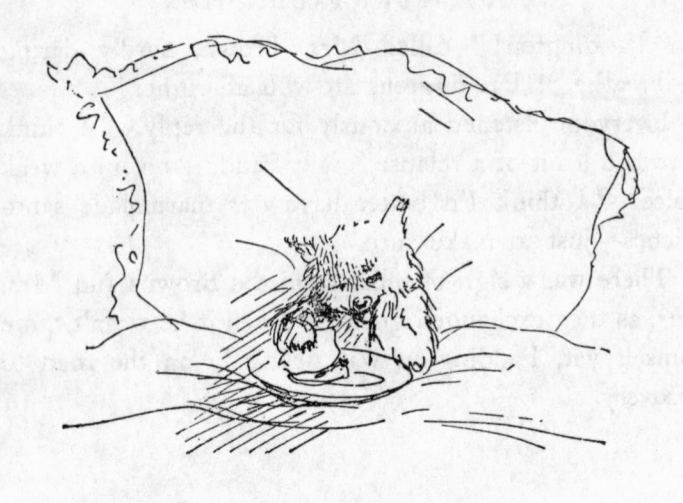

"Mercy me, no," said Mrs. Bird, fanning herself with the morning paper. "That's what I'm trying to tell you. He's much better. He's sitting up in bed asking for a marmalade sandwich!"

"A marmalade sandwich?" exclaimed Mrs. Brown. "Oh, thank goodness!" She wasn't quite sure whether she wanted to laugh or cry. "I never knew hearing the word marmalade could make me feel so happy."

Just as she spoke there was a loud ring from the bell which Mr. Brown had installed by the side of Paddington's bed in case of emergency.

"Oh dear," exclaimed Mrs. Bird. "I hope I haven't spoken too soon!" She rushed out of the room and everyone followed her up the stairs to Paddington's room. When they entered, Paddington was lying on his back with his paws in the air, staring up at the ceiling.

"Paddington!" called Mrs. Brown, hardly daring to breathe. "Paddington, are you all right?"

Everyone listened anxiously for the reply. "I think I've had a bit of a relapse," said Paddington, in a weak voice. "I think I'd better have *two* marmalade sandwiches—just to make sure."

There was a sigh of relief from the Browns and Mrs. Bird as they exchanged glances. Even if he wasn't quite himself yet, Paddington was definitely on the road to recovery.

Paddington and the Christmas Shopping

"I suppose I shouldn't say it," remarked Mrs. Bird, "but I shall be glad when Christmas is over."

The few weeks before Christmas were usually busy ones for Mrs. Bird. There were so many mince-pies, puddings and cakes to be made that much of her time was spent in the kitchen. This year matters hadn't been helped by the fact that Paddington was at home for most of the day "convalescing" after his illness. Paddington was very interested in mince-pies, and if he

had opened the oven door once to see how they were getting on, he'd done it a dozen times.

Paddington's convalescence had been a difficult time for the Browns. While he had remained in bed it had been bad enough, because he kept getting grape-pips all over the sheets. But if anything, matters had got worse once he was up and about. He wasn't very good at " doing nothing " and it had become a full time occupation keeping him amused and out of trouble. He had even had several goes at knitting something—no one ever quite knew what—but he'd got in such a tangle with the wool, and it had become so sticky with marmalade, that in the end they had to throw it away. Even the dustman had said some very nasty things about it when he came to collect the rubbish.

" He seems very quiet at the moment," said Mrs. Brown. " I think he's busy with his Christmas list."

" You're not *really* taking him shopping with you this afternoon, are you? " asked Mrs. Bird. " You know what happened last time."*

Mrs. Brown sighed. She had vivid memories of the last time she had taken Paddington shopping. " I can't *not* take him," she said. " I did promise and he's been looking forward to it so much."

Paddington liked shopping. He always enjoyed looking in the shop windows and since he had read in the paper about all the Christmas decorations, he had thought of very little else. Besides, he had a special

* See *A Bear Called Paddington*

reason for wanting to go shopping this time. Although he hadn't told anyone, Paddington had been saving hard for some while in order to buy the Browns and his other friends some presents.

He had already bought a frame for his picture and sent it, together with a large jar of honey, to his Aunt Lucy in Peru, because presents for overseas had to be posted early.

He had several lists marked "SEACRET" which were locked away in his case, and he had been keeping his ears open for some time listening to conversation in the hope of finding something they all needed.

"Anyway," said Mrs. Brown, "it's so nice having him around again, and he's been so good lately, I think he ought to have a treat."

"Besides," she added, "I'm not taking him to Barkridges this time—I'm taking him to Crumbold and Ferns."

Mrs. Bird put down her baking tray. "Are you sure you're doing the right thing taking him there?" she exclaimed. "You know what they're like."

Crumbold and Ferns was a very old established shop where everyone spoke in whispers and all the assistants wore frock-coats. Only the best people went to Crumbold and Ferns.

"It's Christmas," said Mrs. Brown, recklessly. "It'll be a nice treat for him."

And when Paddington set off with Mrs. Brown after lunch, even Mrs. Bird had to admit he looked smart

enough to go anywhere. His duffle coat, which had just come back from the cleaners, was spotlessly clean, and even his old hat—which Paddington always insisted on wearing when he went on shopping expeditions— looked unusually neat.

All the same, as Paddington waved his paw at the corner, and Mrs. Bird turned to go back indoors, she couldn't help feeling glad she was staying at home.

Paddington enjoyed the journey to Crumbold and Ferns. They went by bus and he managed to get a front seat downstairs. By standing on the seat he could just see through the little hole in the screen behind the driver's back. Paddington tapped on the glass several times and waved his paw at the man behind the wheel, but he was much too busy with the traffic to look round— in fact they drove a long way without stopping at all.

The conductor was cross when he saw what Padding- ton was doing. " Oi! " he shouted. " Stop that there tapping! It's bears like you what get buses a bad name. We've gone past three queues already."

But he was a kindly man and when Paddington said he was sorry, he explained to him all about the signals for making buses stop or go on, and he gave him the end of a roll of tickets as a present. When he had col- lected all the fares, he came back again and pointed out some buildings of interest to Paddington as they passed them. He even presented him with a large bullseye which he found in his money bag. Paddington liked seeing new places and he was sorry when the journey

came to an end and he had to say good-bye to the conductor.

There was another slight upset when they reached Crumbold and Ferns. Paddington had an accident with the revolving door. It wasn't really his fault, but he tried to follow Mrs. Brown into the store just as a very distinguished-looking gentleman with a beard came out the other side. The man was in a great hurry and when he pushed the revolving door it started going round at great speed, taking Paddington with it. He went round several times until he found to his astonishment that he was outside on the pavement once more.

He had a brief glimpse of the man with the beard waving to him from the back of a large car as it drove away. The man also appeared to be shouting something, but Paddington never knew what it was, for at that moment he trod on something sharp and fell over backwards again.

He sat in the middle of the pavement examining his foot and found to his surprise that it had a tie-pin sticking in it. Paddington knew it was a tie-pin because Mr. Brown had one very like it—except that his was quite ordinary, whereas this one had something big and shiny fixed to the middle of it. Paddington pinned it to the front of his duffle coat for safety and then suddenly became aware that someone was speaking to him.

"Are you all right, sir?" It was the doorkeeper—a very dignified man in a smart uniform with lots of medals.

"I think so, thank you," said Paddington, as he stood up and dusted himself, "but I've lost my bullseye somewhere."

"Your bullseye?" said the man. "Dear me!" If he felt surprised he showed no signs of it. Doorkeepers at Crumbold and Ferns were always very well trained. All the same, he couldn't help wondering about Paddington. When he noticed the tie-pin with the enormous diamond in the middle, he realised at once that he was dealing with someone very important. "Probably one of these society bears," he thought to himself. But when he caught sight of Paddington's old hat he wasn't quite so sure. "Perhaps he's a huntin', shootin' and fishin' bear up from the country for the day," he decided. "Or even a society bear that's seen better days."

So he held up the passers-by with a stern wave of the hand while they searched the pavement. As he guided Paddington back through the revolving door to Mrs. Brown, who was waiting anxiously on the other side, he tried hard to look as if helping a young bear of quality find his bullseye was an everyday event at Crumbold and Ferns.

Paddington returned his salute with a wave of the paw and then looked around. The inside of the shop was most impressive. Everywhere they went, tall men in frock-coats bowed low and wished them good afternoon. Paddington's paw was quite tired by the time they reached the Household department.

As they both had some secret shopping to do, Mrs.

Brown left Paddington with the assistant and arranged to meet him outside the entrance to the shop in a quarter of an hour.

The man assured Mrs. Brown that Paddington would be quite safe. "Although I don't recall any actual bears," he said, when she explained that Paddington came from Darkest Peru, "we have a number of very distinguished foreign gentlemen among our clients. Many of them do all their Christmas shopping here."

He turned and looked down at Paddington as Mrs. Brown left, brushing an imaginary speck of dust from his frock-coat.

Secretly Paddington was feeling rather overawed by Crumbold and Ferns, and not wishing to disgrace Mrs. Brown by doing the wrong thing, he gave his own coat a passing tap with his paw. The assistant watched with fascination as a small cloud of dust rose into the air and then slowly settled on his nice, clean counter.

Paddington followed the man's gaze. "I expect it came off the pavement," he said, by way of explanation. "I had an accident in the revolving door."

The man coughed. "Oh dear," he said. "How very unfortunate." He gave Paddington a sickly smile and decided to ignore the whole matter. "And what can we do for you, sir?" he asked, brightly.

Paddington looked round carefully to make sure Mrs. Brown was nowhere in sight. "I want a clothes line," he announced.

"A *what?*" exclaimed the assistant.

Paddington hurriedly moved the bullseye to the other side of his mouth. " A clothes line," he repeated, in a muffled voice. " It's for Mrs. Bird. Her old one broke the other day."

The assistant swallowed hard. He found it impossible to understand what this extraordinary young bear was saying.

" Perhaps," he suggested, for a Crumbold and Ferns assistant rarely bent down, " you wouldn't mind standing on the counter? "

Paddington sighed. It really was most difficult trying to explain things sometimes. Climbing up on to the counter he unlocked his suitcase and withdrew an advertisement which he'd cut from Mr. Brown's newspaper several days before.

" Ah! " The assistant's face cleared. " You mean one of our special *expanding* clothes lines, sir." He reached up to a shelf and picked out a small green box. " A very suitable choice, if I may say so, sir. As befits a young bear of taste. I can thoroughly recommend it."

The man pulled a piece of rope through a hole in the side of the box and handed it to Paddington. " This type of expanding clothes line is used by some of the best families in the country."

Paddington looked suitably impressed as he climbed down, holding on to the rope with his paw.

" You see," continued the man, bending over the counter, " it is all quite simple. The clothes line is all contained inside this box. As you walk away with the

226

rope, it unwinds itself. Then, when you have finished with it, you simply turn this handle and . . ." A puzzled note came into his voice.

"You simply turn this handle," he repeated, trying again. Really, it was all most annoying. Instead of the clothes line going back into the box as it was supposed to, more was actually coming out.

"I'm extremely sorry, sir," he began, looking up from the counter. "Something seems to have jammed. . . ." His voice trailed away and a worried look came into his eyes, for Paddington was nowhere in sight.

"I say," he called, to another assistant farther along the counter. "Have you seen a young bear gentleman go past—pulling on a clothes line?"

"He went that way," replied the other man, briefly. He pointed towards the china department. "I think he got caught in the crowd."

"Oh dear," said Paddington's assistant, as he picked up the green box and began pushing his way through the crowd of shoppers, following the trail of the clothes line. "Oh dear! Oh dear!"

As it happened, the assistant wasn't the only one to feel worried. At the other end of the clothes line Paddington was already in trouble. Crumbold and Ferns was filled with people doing their Christmas shopping, and none of them seemed to have time for a small bear. Several times he'd had to crawl under a table in order to avoid being trodden on.

It was a very good clothes line, and Paddington felt
sure Mrs. Bird would like it. But he couldn't help
wishing he'd chosen something else. There seemed to
be no end to it, and he kept getting it tangled round
people's legs.

He went on and on, round a table laden with cups and
saucers, past a pillar, underneath another table, and still
the clothes line trailed after him. All the time the crowd
was getting thicker and thicker and Paddington had to
push hard to make any headway at all. Once or twice he
nearly lost his hat.

Just as he had almost given up hope of ever finding
his way back to the Household department again, he
caught sight of the assistant. To Paddington's surprise,

the man was sitting on the floor, looking very red in the face. His hair was all ruffled and he appeared to be struggling with a table leg.

"Ah, there you are!" he gasped, when he caught sight of Paddington. "I suppose you realise, young bear, I've been following you all round the china department. Now you've tied everything up in knots."

"Oh dear," said Paddington, looking at the rope.

"Did *I* do that? I'm afraid I got lost. Bears aren't very good in crowds, you know. I must have gone under the same table twice."

"What have you done with the other end?" shouted the assistant.

He wasn't in the best of tempers. It was hot and noisy under the table and people kept kicking him. Apart from that, it was most undignified.

"It's here," said Paddington, trying to find his end of the rope. "At least—it was a moment ago."

"Where?" shouted the assistant. He didn't know whether it was simply the noise of the crowd, but he still couldn't understand a word this young bear uttered. Whenever he did say anything it seemed to be accompanied by a strange crunching noise and a strong smell of peppermint.

"Speak up," he shouted, cupping a hand to his ear. "I can't hear a word you say."

Paddington looked at the man uneasily. He looked rather cross and he was beginning to wish he had left his bullseye on the pavement outside. It was a very nice bullseye but it made talking most difficult.

It was as he felt in his duffle coat pocket for a handkerchief that it happened.

The assistant jumped slightly and the expression on his face froze and then gradually changed to one of disbelief.

"Excuse me," said Paddington, tapping him on the

shoulder, " but I think my bullseye has fallen in your ear! "

" Your *bullseye*? " exclaimed the man, in a horrified tone of voice. " Fallen in my ear? "

" Yes," said Paddington. " It was given to me by a bus conductor and I'm afraid it's got a bit slippery where I've been sucking it."

The assistant crawled out from under the table and drew himself up to his full height. With a look of great distaste, he withdrew the remains of Paddington's bullseye from his ear. He held it for a moment between thumb and forefinger and then hurriedly placed it on a nearby counter. It was bad enough having to crawl around the floor untangling a clothes line—but to have a bullseye in his ear—such a thing had never been known before in Crumbold and Ferns.

He took a deep breath and pointed a trembling finger in Paddington's direction. But as he opened his mouth to speak he noticed that Paddington was no longer there. Neither, for that matter, was the clothes line. He was only just in time to grab the table as it rocked on its legs. As it was, several plates and a cup and saucer fell to the floor.

The assistant raised his eyes to the ceiling and made a mental note to avoid any young bears who came into the shop in future.

There seemed to be a commotion going on in the direction of the entrance hall. He had his own ideas on the possible cause of it, but wisely he decided to keep

his thoughts to himself. He had had quite enough to do with bear customers for one day.

Mrs. Brown pushed her way through the crowd which had formed on the pavement outside Crumbold and Ferns.

"Excuse me," she said, pulling on the doorkeeper's sleeve. "Excuse me. You haven't seen a young bear in a blue duffle coat, have you? We arranged to meet here and there are so many people about I'm really rather worried."

The doorkeeper touched his cap. "That wouldn't be the young gentleman in question, ma'am?" he asked, pointing through a gap in the crowd to where another man in uniform was struggling with the revolving door. "If it is—he's stuck! Good and proper. Can't get in and can't get out. Right in the middle he is, so to speak."

"Oh dear," said Mrs. Brown. "That certainly sounds as if it might be Paddington."

Standing on tip-toe, she peered over the shoulder of a bearded gentleman in front of her. The man was shouting words of encouragement as he tapped on the glass and she just caught a glimpse of a familiar paw as it waved back in acknowledgment.

"It *is* Paddington," she exclaimed. "Now how on earth did he get in there?"

"Ah," said the doorkeeper. "That's just what we're trying to find out. Something to do with 'is getting a clothes line wrapped round the 'inges, so they say."

232

There was a ripple of excitement from the crowd as the door started to revolve once more.

Everyone made a rush for Paddington, but the distinguished man with the beard reached him first. To everyone's surprise, he took hold of his paw and began pumping it up and down.

"Thank you, bear," he kept saying. "Glad to know you, bear!"

"Glad to know *you*," repeated Paddington, looking as surprised as anyone.

"I say," exclaimed the doorkeeper respectfully, as he turned to Mrs. Brown. "I didn't know he was a friend of Sir Gresholm Gibbs."

"Neither did I," said Mrs. Brown. "And who might Sir Gresholm Gibbs be?"

"Sir Gresholm," repeated the doorkeeper, in a hushed voice. "Why, he's a famous millionaire. He's one of Crumbold and Ferns' most important customers."

He pushed back the crowd of interested spectators to allow Paddington and the distinguished man a free passage.

"Dear lady," said Sir Gresholm, bowing low as he approached. "You must be Mrs. Brown. I've just been hearing all about you."

"Oh?" said Mrs. Brown, doubtfully.

"This young bear of yours found a most valuable diamond tie-pin which I lost earlier this afternoon," said Sir Gresholm. "Not only that, but he's kept it in safe custody all this time."

233

"A diamond tie-pin?" exclaimed Mrs. Brown, looking at Paddington. It was the first she had heard of any diamond tie-pin.

"I found it when I lost my bullseye," said Paddington, in a loud stage whisper.

"An example to us all," boomed Sir Gresholm, as he turned to the crowd and pointed at Paddington.

Paddington waved a paw modestly in the air as one or two people applauded.

"And now, dear lady," continued Sir Gresholm, turning to Mrs. Brown. "I understand you intend showing this young bear some of the Christmas decorations."

"Well," said Mrs. Brown. "I was hoping to. He hasn't seen them before and it's really his first trip out since he was ill."

"In that case," said Sir Gresholm, waving to a luxurious car which was parked by the side of the pavement. "my car is at your disposal."

"Ooh," said Paddington. "Is it really?" His eyes glistened. He'd never seen such an enormous car before, let alone ever dreamt of riding in one.

"Yes, indeed," said Sir Gresholm, as he held the door open for them. "That is," he added, as he noticed a worried expression cross Paddington's face, "if you would do me the honour."

"Oh, yes," said Paddington, politely. "I would like to do you the honour very much indeed." He

hesitated. "But I've left my bullseye on one of the counters in Crumbold and Ferns."

"Oh dear," said the gentleman, as he helped Paddington and Mrs. Brown into the car. "Then there's only one thing we can do."

He tapped on the glass window behind the driver

with his stick. "Drive on, James," he said. "And don't stop until we reach the nearest sweet shop."

"One with bullseyes, please, Mr. James," called Paddington.

"Definitely one with bullseyes," repeated Sir Gresholm. "That's most important." He turned to Mrs. Brown with a twinkle in his eye. "You know," he said, "I'm looking forward to this."

"So am I," said Paddington earnestly, as he gazed out of the window at all the lights.

As the huge car drew away from the kerb he stood on the seat and gave a final wave of his paw to the crowd of open-mouthed spectators, and then settled back, holding on to a long gold tassel with his other paw.

It wasn't every day a bear was able to ride round London in such a magnificent car and Paddington wanted to enjoy it to the full.

CHAPTER SEVEN

Christmas

PADDINGTON FOUND that Christmas took a long time to come. Each morning when he hurried downstairs he crossed the date off the calendar, but the more days he crossed off the farther away it seemed.

However, there was plenty to occupy his mind. For one thing, the postman started arriving later and later in the morning, and when he did finally reach the Browns' house there were so many letters to deliver he had a job to push them all through the letter-box. Often there were mysterious-looking parcels as well, which Mrs. Bird promptly hid before Paddington had time to squeeze them.

237

A surprising number of the envelopes were addressed to Paddington himself, and he carefully made a list of all those who had sent him Christmas cards so that he could be sure of thanking them.

"You may be only a small bear," said Mrs. Bird, as she helped him arrange the cards on the mantelpiece, "but you certainly leave your mark."

Paddington wasn't sure how to take this especially as Mrs. Bird had just polished the hall floor, but when he examined his paws they were quite clean.

Paddington had made his own Christmas cards. Some he had drawn himself, decorating the edges with holly and mistletoe; others had been made out of pictures cut from Mrs. Brown's magazines. But each one had the words A MERRY CHRISTMAS AND A HAPPY NEW YEAR printed on the front, and they were signed PADINGTUN BROWN on the inside—together with his special paw mark to show that they were genuine.

Paddington wasn't sure about the spelling of A MERRY CHRISTMAS. It didn't look at all right. But Mrs. Bird checked all the words in a dictionary for him to make certain.

"I don't suppose many people get Christmas cards from a bear," she explained. "They'll probably want to keep them, so you ought to make sure they are right."

One evening Mr. Brown arrived home with a huge Christmas tree tied to the roof of his car. It was placed in a position of honour by the dining-room window and both Paddington and Mr. Brown spent a long

time decorating it with coloured electric lights and silver tinsel.

Apart from the Christmas tree, there were paper chains and holly to be put up, and large coloured bells made of crinkly paper. Paddington enjoyed doing the paper chains. He managed to persuade Mr. Brown that bears were very good at putting up decorations and together they did most of the house, with Paddington standing on Mr. Brown's shoulders while Mr. Brown handed up the drawing pins. It came to an unhappy end one evening when Paddington accidentally put his paw on a drawing pin which he'd left on top of Mr. Brown's head. When Mrs. Bird rushed into the dining-room to see what all the fuss was about, and to inquire why all the lights had suddenly gone out, she found Paddington hanging by his paws from the chandelier and Mr. Brown dancing round the room rubbing his head.

But by then the decorations were almost finished and the house had taken on quite a festive air. The sideboard was groaning under the weight of nuts and oranges, dates and figs, none of which Paddington was allowed to touch, and Mr. Brown had stopped smoking his pipe and was filling the air instead with the smell of cigars.

The excitement in the Browns' house mounted, until it reached fever pitch a few days before Christmas, when Jonathan and Judy arrived home for the holidays.

But if the days leading up to Christmas were busy and

exciting, they were nothing compared with Christmas day itself.

The Browns were up early on Christmas morning—much earlier than they had intended. It all started when Paddington woke to find a large pillow case at the bottom of his bed. His eyes nearly popped out with astonishment when he switched his torch on, for it was bulging with parcels, and it certainly hadn't been there when he'd gone to bed on Christmas Eve.

Paddington's eyes grew larger and larger as he unwrapped the brightly coloured paper round each present. A few days before, on Mrs. Bird's instructions, he had made a list of all the things he hoped to have given him and had hidden it up one of the chimneys. It was a strange thing, but everything on that list seemed to be in the pillow case.

There was a large chemistry outfit from Mr. Brown, full of jars and bottles and test tubes, which looked very interesting. And there was a miniature xylophone from Mrs. Brown, which pleased him no end. Paddington was fond of music—especially the loud sort, which was good for conducting—and he had always wanted something he could actually play.

Mrs. Bird's parcel was even more exciting, for it contained a checked cap which he'd especially asked for and had underlined on his list. Paddington stood on the end of his bed, admiring the effect in the mirror for quite a while.

Jonathan and Judy had each given him a travel book. Paddington was very interested in geography, being a much-travelled bear, and he was pleased to see there were plenty of maps and coloured pictures inside.

The noise from Paddington's room was soon sufficient to waken both Jonathan and Judy, and in no time at all the whole house was in an uproar, with wrapping paper and bits of string everywhere.

" I'm as patriotic as the next man," grumbled Mr. Brown. " But I draw the line when bears start playing the National Anthem at six o'clock in the morning— especially on a xylophone."

As always, it was left to Mrs. Bird to restore order. " No more presents until after lunch," she said, firmly. She had just tripped over Paddington on the upstairs landing, where he was investigating his new chemical outfit, and something nasty had gone in one of her slippers.

" It's all right, Mrs. Bird," said Paddington, con- sulting his instruction book, " it's only some iron filings. I don't think they're dangerous."

" Dangerous or not," said Mrs. Bird " I've a big dinner to cook—not to mention your birthday cake to finish decorating."

Being a bear, Paddington had two birthdays each year—one in the summer and one at Christmas—and the Browns were holding a party in his honour to which Mr. Gruber had been invited.

After they'd had breakfast and been to church, the

morning passed quickly and Paddington spent most of his time trying to decide what to do next. With so many things from which to choose it was most difficult. He read some chapters from his books and made several interesting smells and a small explosion with his chemical outfit.

Mr. Brown was already in trouble for having given it to him, especially when Paddington found a chapter in the instruction book headed " Indoor Fireworks." He made himself a " never ending " snake which wouldn't stop growing and frightened Mrs. Bird to death when she met it coming down the stairs.

" If we don't watch out," she confided to Mrs. Brown, " we shan't last over Christmas. We shall either be blown to smithereens or poisoned. He was testing my gravy with some litmus paper just now."

Mrs. Brown sighed. " It's a good job Christmas only comes once a year," she said, as she helped Mrs. Bird with the potatoes.

" It isn't over yet," warned Mrs. Bird.

Fortunately, Mr. Gruber arrived at that moment and some measure of order was established before they all sat down to dinner.

Paddington's eyes glistened as he surveyed the table. He didn't agree with Mr. Brown when he said it all looked too good to eat. All the same, even Paddington got noticeably slower towards the end when Mrs. Bird brought in the Christmas pudding.

" Well," said Mr. Gruber, a few minutes later, as he

sat back and surveyed his empty plate, " I must say that's the best Christmas dinner I've had for many a day. Thank you very much indeed! "

" Hear! Hear! " agreed Mr. Brown. " What do you say, Paddington? "

" It was very nice," said Paddington, licking some cream from his whiskers. " Except I had a bone in my Christmas pudding."

" You *what?* " exclaimed Mrs. Brown. " Don't be silly—there are no bones in Christmas pudding."

" I had one," said Paddington, firmly. " It was all hard—and it stuck in my throat."

" Good gracious! " exclaimed Mrs. Bird. " The sixpence! I always put a piece of silver in the Christmas pudding."

" What! " said Paddington, nearly falling off his chair. " A sixpence? I've never heard of a sixpence pudding before."

" Quick," shouted Mr. Brown, rising to the emergency. " Turn him upside down."

Before Paddington could reply, he found himself hanging head downwards while Mr. Brown and Mr. Gruber took it in turns to shake him. The rest of the family stood round watching the floor.

" It's no good," said Mr. Brown, after a while. " It must have gone too far." He helped Mr. Gruber lift Paddington into an armchair where he lay gasping for breath.

" I've got a magnet upstairs," said Jonathan. " We

could try lowering it down his throat on a piece of string."

" I don't think so, dear," said Mrs. Brown, in a worried tone of voice. " He might swallow that and then we should be even worse off." She bent over the chair. " How do you feel, Paddington?"

" Sick," said Paddington, in an aggrieved tone of voice.

" Of course you do, dear," said Mrs. Brown. " It's only to be expected. There's only one thing to do— we shall have to send for the doctor."

" Thank goodness I scrubbed it first," said Mrs. Bird. " It might have been covered with germs."

" But I *didn't* swallow it," gasped Paddington. " I only nearly did. Then I put it on the side of my plate. I didn't know it was a sixpence because it was all covered with Christmas pudding."

Paddington felt very fed up. He'd just eaten one of the best dinners he could ever remember and now he'd been turned upside down and shaken without even being given time to explain.

Everyone exchanged glances and then crept quietly away, leaving Paddington to recover by himself. There didn't seem to be much they *could* say.

But after the dinner things had been cleared away, and by the time Mrs. Bird had made some strong coffee, Paddington was almost himself again. He was sitting up in the chair helping himself to some dates when they

244

trooped back into the room. It took a lot to make Paddington ill for very long.

When they had finished their coffee, and were sitting round the blazing fire feeling warm and comfortable, Mr. Brown rubbed his hands. " Now, Paddington," he said, " it's not only Christmas, it's your birthday as well. What would you like to do? "

A mysterious expression came over Paddington's face. " If you all go in the other room," he announced, " I've a special surprise for you."

" Oh dear, *must* we, Paddington? " said Mrs. Brown. " There isn't a fire."

" I shan't be long," said Paddington, firmly. " But it's a special surprise and it has to be prepared." He held the door open and the Browns, Mrs. Bird and Mr. Gruber filed obediently into the other room.

" Now close your eyes," said Paddington, when they were all settled, " and I'll let you know when I'm ready."

Mrs. Brown shivered. " I hope you won't be too long," she called. But the only reply was the sound of the door clicking shut.

They waited for several minutes without speaking, and then Mr. Gruber cleared his throat. " Do you think young Mr. Brown's forgotten about us? " he asked.

" I don't know," said Mrs. Brown. " But I'm not waiting much longer."

" Henry! " she exclaimed, as she opened her eyes. " Have you gone to sleep? "

" Er, wassat? " snorted Mr. Brown. He had eaten such a large dinner he was finding it difficult to keep awake. " What's happening? Have I missed anything? "

" Nothing's happening," said Mrs. Brown. " Henry, you'd better go and see what Paddington's up to."

Several more minutes went by before Mr. Brown returned to announce that he couldn't find Paddington anywhere.

" Well, he must be *somewhere*," said Mrs. Brown. " Bears don't disappear into thin air."

" Crikey! " exclaimed Jonathan, as a thought suddenly struck him. " You don't think he's playing at Father Christmas, do you? He was asking all about it the other day when he put his list up the chimney. I bet that's why he wanted us to come in here—because this chimney connects with the one upstairs—and there isn't a fire."

" Father Christmas? " said Mr. Brown. " I'll give him Father Christmas! " He stuck his head up the chimney and called Paddington's name several times. " I can't see anything," he said, striking a match. As if in answer a large lump of soot descended and burst on top of his head.

" Now look what you've done, Henry," said Mrs. Brown. " Shouting so—you've disturbed the soot. All over your clean shirt!"

" If it *is* young Mr. Brown, perhaps he's stuck somewhere," suggested Mr. Gruber. " He did have rather

a large dinner. I remember wondering at the time where he put it all."

Mr. Gruber's suggestion had an immediate effect on the party and everyone began to look serious.

" Why, he might suffocate with the fumes," exclaimed Mrs. Bird, as she hurried outside to the broom cupboard.

When she returned, armed with a mop, everyone took it in turns to poke it up the chimney but even though they strained their ears they couldn't hear a sound.

It was while the excitement was at its height that Paddington came into the room. He looked most surprised when he saw Mr. Brown with his head up the chimney.

"You can come into the dining-room now," he announced, looking round the room. "I've finished wrapping my presents and they're all on the Christmas tree."

"You don't mean to say," spluttered Mr. Brown, as he sat in the fireplace rubbing his face with a handkerchief, "you've been in the other room all the time?"

"Yes," said Paddington, innocently. "I hope I didn't keep you waiting too long."

Mrs. Brown looked at her husband. "I thought you said you'd looked everywhere," she exclaimed.

"Well—we'd just come from the dining-room," said Mr. Brown, looking very sheepish. "I didn't think he'd be *there*."

"It only goes to show," said Mrs. Bird hastily, as she caught sight of the expression on Mr. Brown's face, "how easy it is to give a bear a bad name."

Paddington looked most interested when they explained to him what all the fuss was about.

"I never thought of coming down the chimney," he said, staring at the fireplace.

"Well, you're not thinking about it now either," replied Mr. Brown, sternly.

But even Mr. Brown's expression changed as he

followed Paddington into the dining-room and saw the surprise that had been prepared for them.

In addition to the presents that had already been placed on the tree, there were now six newly wrapped ones tied to the lower branches. If the Browns recognised the wrapping paper they had used for Paddington's presents earlier in the day, they were much too polite to say anything.

" I'm afraid I had to use old paper," said Paddington apologetically, as he waved a paw at the tree. " I hadn't any money left. That's why you had to go in the other room while I wrapped them."

" Really, Paddington," said Mrs. Brown. " I'm very cross with you—spending all your money on presents for us."

" I'm afraid they're rather ordinary," said Paddington, as he settled back in a chair to watch the others. " But I hope you like them. They're all labelled so that you know which is which."

" Ordinary? " exclaimed Mr. Brown, as he opened his parcel. " I don't call a pipe rack ordinary. And there's an ounce of my favourite tobacco tied to the back as well! "

" Gosh! A new stamp album! " cried Jonathan. " Whizzo! And it's got some stamps inside already."

" They're Peruvian ones from Aunt Lucy's postcards," said Paddington. " I've been saving them for you."

" And I've got a box of paints," exclaimed Judy.

249

" Thank you very much, Paddington. It's just what I wanted."

" We all seem to be lucky," said Mrs. Brown, as she unwrapped a parcel containing a bottle of her favourite lavender water. " How *did* you guess? I finished my last bottle only a week ago."

" I'm sorry about your parcel, Mrs. Bird," said Paddington, looking across the room. " I had a bit of a job with the knots."

" It must be something special," said Mr. Brown. " It seems all string and no parcel."

" That's because it's really clothes line," explained Paddington, " not string. I rescued it when I got stuck in the revolving door at Crumbold and Ferns."

" That makes two presents in one," said Mrs. Bird, as she freed the last of the knots and began unwinding yards and yards of paper. " How exciting. I can't think what it can be."

" Why," she exclaimed. " I do believe it's a brooch! And it's shaped like a bear—how lovely! " Mrs. Bird looked most touched as she handed the present round for everyone to see. " I shall keep it in a safe place," she added, " and only wear it on special occasions— when I want to impress people."

" I don't know what mine is," said Mr. Gruber, as they all turned to him. He squeezed the parcel. " It's such a funny shape."

" It's a drinking mug! " he exclaimed, his face

lighting up with pleasure. " And it even has my name painted on the side! "

" It's for your elevenses, Mr. Gruber," said Paddington. " I noticed your old one was getting rather chipped."

" I'm sure it will make my cocoa taste better than it ever has before," said Mr. Gruber.

He stood up and cleared his throat. " I think I would like to offer a vote of thanks to young Mr. Brown," he said, " for all his nice presents. I'm sure he must have given them a great deal of thought."

" Hear! Hear! " echoed Mr. Brown, as he filled his pipe.

Mr. Gruber felt under his chair. " And while I think of it, Mr. Brown, I have a small present for you."

Everyone stood round and watched while Paddington struggled with his parcel, eager to see what Mr. Gruber had bought him. A gasp of surprise went up as he tore the paper to one side, for it was a beautifully bound leather scrapbook, with " Paddington Brown " printed in gold leaf on the cover.

Paddington didn't know what to say, but Mr. Gruber waved his thanks to one side. " I know how you enjoy writing about your adventures, Mr. Brown," he said. " And you have so many I'm sure your present scrapbook must be almost full."

" It is," said Paddington, earnestly. " And I'm sure I shall have lots more. Things happen to me, you know. But I shall only put my best ones in here! "

When he made his way up to bed later that evening, his mind was in such a whirl, and he was so full of good things, he could hardly climb the stairs—let alone think about anything. He wasn't quite sure which he had enjoyed most. The presents, the Christmas dinner, the games, or the tea—with the special marmalade-layer birthday cake Mrs. Bird had made in his honour. Pausing on the corner half-way up, he decided he had enjoyed giving his own presents best of all.

"Paddington! Whatever have you got there?" He jumped and hastily hid his paw behind his back as he heard Mrs. Bird calling from the bottom of the stairs.

"It's only some sixpence pudding, Mrs. Bird," he called, looking over the banisters guiltily. "I thought I might get hungry during the night and I didn't want to take any chances."

"Honestly!" Mrs. Bird exclaimed, as she was joined by the others. "What *does* that bear look like? A paper hat about ten sizes

too big on his head—Mr. Gruber's scrapbook in one paw—and a plate of Christmas pudding in the other!"

"I don't care what he looks like," said Mrs. Brown, "so long as he stays that way. The place wouldn't be the same without him."

But Paddington was too far away to hear what was being said. He was already sitting up in bed, busily writing in his scrapbook.

First of all, there was a very important notice to go on the front page. It said:

PADINGTUN BROWN,

32 WINDSOR GARDENS,

LUNDUN,

ENGLAND,

YUROPE,

THE WORLD.

Then, on the next page he added, in large capital letters: MY ADDVENTURES. CHAPTER WUN.

Paddington sucked his pen thoughtfully for a moment and then carefully replaced the top on the bottle of ink before it had a chance to fall over on the sheets. He felt much too sleepy to write any more. But he didn't really mind. To-morrow was another day—and he felt quite sure he *would* have some more adventures—even if he didn't know what they were going to be as yet.

Paddington lay back and pulled the blankets up round his whiskers. It was warm and comfortable and he sighed contentedly as he closed his eyes. It was nice being a bear. Especially a bear called Paddington.